OUR LAST HOPE

THE FORGOTTEN ROAD TO LIBERTY

BY MICHAEL MAHARREY

PEACE + LIBERTY

ISBN: 0615709877
ISBN-13: 978-0615709871

DEDICATION AND ACKNOWLEDGEMENTS

A few years ago, I was a lot like many of you holding this book: fed up and discouraged.

I spent most of my adult life nibbling around the edges of the political process. I listened to talk radio. I periodically wrote op-eds and blog pieces. I got involved in presidential and congressional campaigns.

And nothing changed.

The federal government kept getting more powerful. The nation spiraled deeper in debt. Individual liberties continued to erode.

Like so many Americans, the financial meltdown of at the end of the G.W. Bush administration really got my attention. In April 2009, I found myself standing in a park in downtown Lexington, Ky. at one of the early Tea Parties rallies. At that point, I realized I needed to do more. I didn't want my kids or grandkids to ask me one day, "Daddy, what did you do when America was in the middle of its collapse?" and find that the only answer I could come up with was "I stood in a park and then I voted."

Around that time, I stumbled upon the Tenth Amendment Center. As I perused the website, I began reading about this principle called "nullification." I'd never heard of such a thing. It sounded radical. A little bit out there. I wasn't quite sure what it was all about. Then one day, I Googled the *Kentucky Resolutions of 1798*. As I read the words of Thomas Jefferson, my entire political worldview shifted.

Since that time, I've become absolutely convinced that the people of the several states must step in and force the federal government back into its proper role if we ever hope to turn the American ship around and bring any semblance of sanity to Washington D.C. Uncle Sam will never willingly give up all of the power he's accumulated over the last 100 years. We have to take it back.

Nullification provides the tool.

But the very mention of the "n-word" causes wailing and gnashing of teeth. Resistance to the idea comes from the left, the right and the middle. Some call it unconstitutional. Some call it unwarranted rebellion. Some call it racist.

I call it our last hope.

We've tried begging our congressional representatives and senators to roll back unconstitutional acts. They ignored us. We've tried suing in court. They ruled against us. We've tried voting the bums out. We ended up with a new set of bums.

Wash, rinse and repeat.

It's time to try something different.

The book in your hand culminates nearly two years of research and study. Hopefully, it will serve as a good introduction to the moral, philosophical and historical case for nullification. I am not a historian or an academic. I am a journalist by training. So gathering information from lots of sources, compiling it and making it easy to understand is what I do best. Hopefully, I've accomplished that. This book is not meant to serve as the final word on the subject of nullification. It's really just the first stepping stone onto a long path. I hope it will be a jumping-off point for you, directing you to a deeper study of the subject.

My name is on the front cover, but the work and input of many others went into it. I owe a great debt of gratitude to many people who helped make this book possible.

First, I want to thank Tom Woods. His book, *Nullification: How to Resist Federal Tyranny in the 21st Century,* put nullification back in the public spotlight. If you haven't read it, make sure you do. He meticulously lays out the historical case for nullification, and his academic work serves as the foundation for my own. I have benefitted greatly from our conversations and correspondence, and this book would not have been possible without his trailblazing efforts.

When I told Tenth Amendment Center founder and executive director Michael Boldin that I wanted to write a book on nullification, he said, "Go for it." Michael has a way of making a person believe in his own abilities. I am deeply grateful that he saw fit to bring me into the TAC family, and I appreciate his willingness to put the organization's name on this book.

Lesley Swann served as my primary editor. Her attention to detail and poignant suggestions helped transform a rough manuscript into a polished finished product. A big thank you goes out to Lesley for all of her hard work and input.

Thanks also to William Kennedy. He gave the manuscript a read as well, suggested numerous edits and helped me clarify several points.

The biggest thank you goes out to my wife Cynthia. I simply could not have done this without her love and support. I can't tell you how many times she had to put up with me interrupting whatever she was doing so I could run some arcane idea past her. Or how often she had to act interested when I enthusiastically read her long passages from Locke or the *Federalist Papers*. Or how valuable her input was when I read her the entire manuscript out loud at our kitchen counter over the course of several weeks. But more than that, she kept me going when I got discouraged or frustrated, and she made me believe that I really could write an entire book.

Finally, I dedicate this book to Sinead, Darian and Brendan. May God grant you the grace to live free.

CONTENTS

PREFACE

A giant fluffy monster ambles down city streets. Vehicles crash as panicked citizens flee in abject horror. A sticky grin splits the marshmallow man's face and he roars in delight while crushing vehicles under his gooey feet.

"Sorry, Venkman; I'm terrified beyond the capacity for rational thought," Dr. Egon Spengler says.

In the 1984 film classic *Ghostbusters*, the villain tells the heroes to choose the form of their destructor, and the ghost busting crew ends up locked in mortal combat with a 100-foot tall Stay Puft Marshmallow Man.

A sweet, tasty treat morphed into a vicious killing machine.

"I tried to think of the most harmless thing – something that I loved from my childhood, something that would never ever possibly destroy us: Mr. Stay Puft," Dr. Raymond Stantz explains to his fellow Ghostbusters.

In an interview, Dan Aykroyd later revealed how he conceived of Mr. Stay Puft as a villain.

"You created this white monster to sell your products, and it seems harmless and puff and cute — but given the right circumstances, everything can be turned back and become evil." (1)

Mr. Stay Puft could easily represent a monster that roams America, across the fruited plane, from sea to shining sea. It hails from Washington D.C. and wraps itself in red white and blue bunting. It bullies, badgers and browbeats citizens to get its way. Over the last 100 years, it grew exponentially, shoving its tentacles into nearly every nook and cranny of American life. Its steely claws grasp everything in sight, scattering about just enough morsels to keep most Americans reasonably placated. Or perhaps they remain too frightened to engage in any rational thought.

A frighteningly giant monster, continually growing.

In 2011, President Obama proposed a budget including more than $3.8 trillion in federal spending, running a deficit eclipsing $1.5 trillion. This added to a national debt already standing at well over $14 trillion. (2)

Fourteen-trillion. Most people can't even conceive this number. If you lined up dollar bills end to end, you could stretch a line of dollars to the moon and back 2,773 times and still have dollars left over.

To put that into perspective, according to National Budget Office figures, the federal government spent $13.6 billion in 1901 (adjusted to 2010 dollars) and ran a 1.6 billion surplus. In other words, the federal government spent more than 292 times in 2011 than it did in 1901 under the budget. That represents true inflation adjusted growth. (3)

The federal government enforces thousands of regulations through hundreds of departments, bureaus and agencies. It mandates everything from toilet tank size to the kind of light bulbs Americans use. The IRS tax code alone fills more than 7,500 printed pages, or for the digitally savvy, more than 24 megabytes. (4) The TSA gropes travelers. OSHA mandates the width between ladder rungs. (Not less than 10 inches (25 cm) apart, nor more than 14 inches (36 cm) apart, as measured between center lines of the rungs, cleats and steps. [5]) And by USDA edict, batter-coated, frozen French fries are considered "fresh vegetables" all across the United States. The federal government employs more than 2 million workers (6) and owns more than 650 million acres of land – nearly 30 percent of the nation's landmass. (7)

Recognizing the need for a mechanism to facilitate common defense, interact with foreign nations and tend to issues of general welfare, the founders created a general government and vested it with limited powers.

James Madison described the role of the federal government in Federalist 45.

> "The powers delegated by the proposed Constitution to the federal government are few and defined. Those which are to remain in the State governments are numerous and indefinite. The former will be exercised principally on external objects, as

war, peace, negotiation and foreign commerce; with which the last the power of taxation will for the most part be connected. The powers reserved to the several States will extend to all objects which, in the ordinary course of affairs, concern the lives, liberties and properties of the people, and the internal order, improvement and prosperity of the State."

Those supporting the new Constitution lobbied for its ratification based on the limited nature of the new government. Many Americans remained unconvinced. They'd just finished fighting a bloody war to free themselves from tyrannical, overreaching government. State ratifiers insisted on amendments to further protect liberty. One of those amendments explicitly expresses the limited scope of federal government.

The powers not delegated to the United States by the Constitution, nor prohibited by it to the States, are reserved to the States respectively, or to the people. – The Tenth Amendment.

Conceived as limited and delegated with enumerated powers for very specific purposes, the United States federal government morphed into an institution with nearly unlimited power, scope and authority. Can anyone rationally look at the behemoth now inhabiting Washington D.C. and argue that the federal government even remotely resembles Madison's vision?

It appears that Aykroyd was correct, "Given the right circumstances, everything can be turned back and become evil."

At his proper size, Mr. Stay Puft was a fun, cuddly, squishy marketing tool for a delicious sweet snack; the kind of character you'd want to send your children outside to play with on a warm sunny day. But at 100-feet tall, he wreaked havoc on an entire city. Realizing his size, power and apparent invincibility, Mr. Stay Puft transformed into a diabolical fiend, taking obvious pleasure in crushing everything around him.

The evil grin said it all.

Similarly, over the last 100 years, our once limited federal government morphed into something frighteningly unrecognizable from the institution originally intended. The feds seek to force Americans into a one-size-fits all health care system, dictate what plants citizens can and cannot grow in their own back yards and conduct armed raids against Amish farmers for the heinous crime of selling raw milk. Heck, even the "peace president" wages war around the globe.

To defeat Mr. Stay Puft, the Ghostbusters had one last hope - cross the energy streams from their proton packs and aim them at Gozer's entrance. The trio destroys Gozer and the marshmallow man in a single mighty explosion, raining marshmallow cream down onto the city streets.

The American people don't need proton packs to obliterate the federal government. As cool as proton packs might be, destruction isn't the objective. The federal government serves important functions, and the United States stand stronger united. But the out of control creature from the Potomac threatens to destroy the very essence of America. We have one last hope. We the people must rein in the monster that the federal government has become. We must shrink it back to its intended size and restrain it within its original delegated powers.

The states hold the key.

The final hope.

Most Americans remember the principle of separated powers from their high school civics class. The founders divided authority between three branches in a system of checks and balances. But few ever learned that the founders intended the states to serve as a check on federal power. James Madison explained how the states could prevent the federal government from overreaching in Federalist 46.

"Should an unwarrantable measure of the federal government be unpopular in particular States, which would seldom fail to be the case, or even a warrantable measure be so, which may sometimes be the case, the means of opposition to it are powerful and at hand. The disquietude of the people; their repugnance and, perhaps refusal to cooperate with

officers of the Union, the frowns of the executive magistracy of the State; the embarrassment created by legislative devices, which would often be added on such occasions, would oppose, in any State, very serious impediments; and were the sentiments of several adjoining States happen to be in Union, would present obstructions which the federal government would hardly be willing to encounter."

The states possess the power and a tool through which to wield it.

Nullification.

The final hope.

Jefferson called it the rightful remedy. Madison called it a state's duty and obligation.

The establishment calls it racist. (More on that later.)

But what exactly is nullification? Do I need a law degree to understand it? Is it really just an early American relic that we should consigned to the dustbin of history? Does a concept first articulated in 1798 really have an application in the 21st century? And why do so many on both the political left and right revolt in horror at the mere mention of the "N" word?

I will answer some of those questions in the following chapters. We'll look at exactly what nullification is, how it's been applied throughout American history and why the critics are wrong. And if you become convinced, as I have, that the states hold the key to restoring our republic to the land of the free, we'll talk a little bit about what you can do to get involved.

So strap on your proton packs and journey with me as we explore ways to bring down Mr. Stay Puft.

1

JUST SAY "NO!"

"Huh?"

A glassy-eyed expression settling somewhere between disbelief and bewilderment. Perhaps some mild head shaking followed by a shoulder shrug.

The typical response to a first-time introduction to the principles of nullification.

Quite frankly, most people just don't seem to get it. At least not initially. That's because most "experts" tend to overcomplicate the concept. The media feeds into this. Read your typical newspaper reporter's explanation of nullification, or listen to pundits discuss the idea on a cable news program, and you'll likely come away with the impression that the principle lurks deep within the shadows, wrapped in some dark, legal mist, penetrable only by scholars with Harvard law degrees and 33 years of constitutional study under their belts.

Perhaps the archaic 18ᵗʰ century language used in the documents that first laid out the principles of nullification contributes to the confusion. Or maybe some folks would rather "We the People" not realize a mechanism to rein in federal power exists, so they try to keep things fuzzy on purpose. Whatever the reason, the impression remains: nullification is a complex legal premise rooted in the minutia of constitutional law.

You wouldn't understand, peasant!

But really, it's not that complicated.

In fact, you can try it at home.

It happens all the time at my house. My wife in particular has developed into an expert in exercising what I like to call "wardrobe nullification." We have two teenage daughters, and wardrobe nullification works something like this: one of my lovely daughters will walk into the room wearing something – shall we say – inappropriate. Perhaps cut a little low. Or maybe riding up a little too high. I generally don't even have a chance to react because my wonderful and gracious wife jumps on it like a hobo on a ham sandwich.

"Oh no, young lady. You are not walking out of this house wearing that. March yourself right back to your room and change those clothes."

And there you have it – nullification.

One-word definition: No!

Here is a simple working definition of nullification for today: any act, or set of actions, that result in a particular law being declared unconstitutional and rendered null, void or even just unenforceable within the borders of a state.

When Congress passed an act stipulating every American must purchase health insurance, multiple states said, "No," passing health care freedom legislation. When the Supreme Court ruled the feds have the authority to make medicinal marijuana illegal across the U.S., did the states shut down their medicinal cannabis programs? No. In fact, more states passed laws legalizing medical marijuana. By the fall of 2012, 17 states ran medical marijuana programs, with several states considering joining that number. They said, "No," defied the federal government and went on with their medical cannabis programs anyway. And when the Bush administration pushed through the Real ID Act in 2005, seeking to create a national system of identification, states said, "No," and refused to take steps to implement the program.

In fact, state governments have utilized nullification to fight a wide range of overreaching federal actions, from military conscription during the War of 1812 to the Fugitive Slave Acts in the 1850s. From overreaching FDA regulations to groping TSA searches today.

Keep in mind; we're not talking about a 3-year-old throwing a temper tantrum, yelling, "No! No! No!" because he didn't get his way. True, in 21st century America, the idea that states can unilaterally declare unconstitutional acts null and void seems radical, even extremist, to many people. And many political pundits would like you to believe that North Dakota declaring the federal health care act unconstitutional is just like a toddler's outburst. Best ignored. Perhaps punished. But nullification sets its roots deep within the Constitutional system envisioned by the framers and ratifiers.

Principles of '98

Nullification wasn't initially advanced by some eccentric, little known political philosopher. In fact, two of the best known Founding Fathers first put quill pen to parchment and articulated the idea – the primary author of the Declaration of Independence and the "Father of the Constitution."

3

Thomas Jefferson and James Madison authored the documents first formally advancing the idea that states could and should intervene when the federal government oversteps its authority in response to the Alien and Sedition Acts passed by Congress in 1798. Jefferson penned resolutions for Kentucky and Madison drafted a similar piece of legislation for the Commonwealth of Virginia. Taken together, the two resolutions lay out what we now call the Principles of '98.

Jefferson summed up the idea simply. When the federal government exercises power not delegated by the Constitution, nullification becomes the "rightful remedy." And Madison insisted state governments have an obligation to protect their citizens.

> "In case of a deliberate, palpable, and dangerous exercise of other powers, not granted by the said compact (the Constitution), the states who are parties thereto, have the right, and are in duty bound, to interpose for arresting the progress of the evil, and for maintaining within their respective limits, the authorities, rights and liberties appertaining to them."

Note Madison's language. He uses the words "palpable," "dangerous" and "evil." He wasn't talking about states ignoring laws they happen to dislike. He wasn't even talking about exercising the power of nullification for minor transgressions. He was addressing egregious violations of the Constitution. Madison expounded on the idea in the Report of 1800, an in-depth defense of the Virginia Resolutions of 1798.

> "It must be a case, not of a light and transient nature, but of a nature dangerous to the great purposes for which the Constitution was established. It must be a case, moreover, not obscure or doubtful in its construction, but plain and palpable."

Jefferson and Madison may have differed slightly on their view as to when states should take action and nullify an act, but both men drew a Constitutional line in the sand.

Whether you go with Jefferson's "whensoever undelegated powers are assumed," or Madison's "deliberate, palpable, and dangerous exercise of other powers," the Alien and Sedition Acts crossed that line.

Four separate laws passed in the summer of 1798 made up the Alien and Sedition Acts. With winds of war blowing across the Atlantic, the Federalist Party majority wrote the laws to prevent "seditious" acts from weakening the U.S. government. Federalists utilized fear to stir up support for these draconian laws, expanding federal power, concentrating authority in the executive branch and severely restricting freedom of speech.

At the time, the U.S. was involved in an undeclared naval war with France. The Quasi-War stemmed from French anger over a treaty opening up trade between the United States and Great Britain and a U.S. refusal to pay Revolutionary War debts after the French Revolution toppled its royal government. American officials argued that since the French government that the U.S. originally borrowed money from no longer existed, the United States was free from the obligation. The conflict raised the ire of many Americans, creating an anti-French backlash. The perceived need to protect America from the French threat provided just the excuse Congress needed to expand federal power. Supporters of the Federalist Party in power harbored political motives as well. The Alien and Sedition Acts provided an avenue to strip power from the minority Democrat-Republican Party.

The Naturalization Act passed on June 18 and extended the amount of time immigrants had to live in the United States before becoming eligible for citizenship form five to 14 years. Like most things political, the stated and the underlying purposes of tightening naturalization requirements were two different things. The law was advanced as a national security measure. But it provided a great benefit to the Federalist Party in power because most recent French and Irish immigrants supported the Democrat-Republican Party.

The Alien Friends Act passed a week later and gave the president sweeping power to deport "dangerous" aliens, in effect elevating the president to the role of judge, jury and "executioner."

> "It shall be lawful for the President of the United States at any time during the continuance of this act, to order all such aliens as he shall judge dangerous to the peace and safety of the United States, or shall have reasonable grounds to suspect are concerned in any treasonable or secret machinations against the government thereof, to depart out of the territory of the United States, within such time as shall be expressed in such order."

Note the wide latitude afforded the president by undefined terms in the act. What constituted "dangerous" and what exactly is a "secret machination?"

On July 6, Congress passed the Alien Enemies Act, allowing for the arrest, imprisonment and deportation of any male citizen of a nation at war with the U.S., even without any evidence that he was an actual threat.

> "All natives, citizens, denizens, or subjects of the hostile nation or government, being males of the age of fourteen years and upwards, who shall be within the United States, and not actually naturalized, shall be liable to be apprehended, restrained, secured and removed, as alien enemies."

The Sedition Act, enacted on July 14, was the most nefarious of the Alien and Sedition Acts. It declared any "treasonable activity" a high misdemeanor punishable by fine and imprisonment. Treasonable activity included "any false, scandalous and malicious writing" against the government or its officials.

> *"If any person shall write, print, utter or publish, or shall cause or procure to be written, printed, uttered or published, or shall knowingly and willingly assist or aid in writing, printing, uttering or publishing any false, scandalous and malicious writing or writings against the government of the United States, or either house of the Congress of the United States, or the President of the United States, with intent to defame the said government, or either house of the said Congress, or the said President, or to bring them, or either of them, into contempt or disrepute; or to excite against them, or either or any of them, the hatred of the good people of the United States, or to stir up sedition within the United States, or to excite any unlawful combinations therein, for opposing or resisting any law of the United States, or any act of the President of the United States, done in pursuance of any such law, or of the powers in him vested by the constitution of the United States, or to resist, oppose, or defeat any such law or act, or to aid, encourage or abet any hostile designs of any foreign nation against the United States, their people or government, then such person, being thereof convicted before any court of the United States having jurisdiction thereof, shall be punished by a fine not exceeding two thousand dollars, and by imprisonment not exceeding two years."*

Notice one notable exception to the list of officials the act forbid disparaging – the vice president. It was presumably permissible under the law to write maliciously about Vice President Thomas Jefferson. He was, after all, a member of the opposition party.

Based on the Sedition Act, federal officials arrested some 25 men, most of them editors of Republican newspapers. There were at least 17 verifiable indictments, 14 under the Sedition Act and three under common law.(1) The Act also effectively shut down many dissenting party presses. Talk about chilling free speech! The Federalists set themselves up to remain permanently in power. How does a candidate campaign to win an election if he can't criticize the incumbent?

This was no "paper tiger" law. The Federalists immediately wielded their new power with great effect.

Benjamin Franklin's grandson was among those prosecuted. Federalists sent "committees of surveillance" to spy on Benjamin Franklin Bache, editor of the *Philadelphia Democrat-Republican Aurora*(2). Bache called the Alien and Sedition Acts an "unconstitutional exercise of power."(3) He was ultimately charged with libeling President John Adams and sedition for his French sympathies. Bache died of yellow fever before he was brought to trial.

During his re-election campaign, U.S. Congressman Matthew Lyon wrote a reply to his Federalist opponents, accusing President Adams of engaging in a "continual grasp for power," having "an unbounded thirst for ridiculous pomp, foolish adulation, and selfish avarice." He was indicted on sedition charges on Oct. 5, 1798, and arrested the next day. A judge fined Matthew $1,000 and sentenced him to four months in prison.(4) Lyon represented Vermont in Congress and also served as the editor of the Republican paper *The Scourge of Aristocracy*. He was reelected to Congress while serving his jail term.

Thomas Cooper, a prominent Pennsylvania lawyer, physician and editor of the *Northumberland Gazette* served six months in prison for criticizing the very law that put him in jail. He wrote an essay laying out his objections to the Alien and Sedition Acts, and criticized President Adams for increasing the size of the army and navy.(5) He was arrested and charged "with having published a false, scandalous and malicious attack on the character of the President of the United States, with an intent to excite the hatred and contempt of the people of this country against the man of their choice."(6)

It doesn't take a constitutional lawyer to recognize the First Amendment violations inherent in the Sedition Acts. In a modern legal climate where even the most obscene speech enjoys protection, we can scarcely imagine federal agents jailing newspaper editors for criticizing government officials. Yet many Americans supported the Alien and Sedition Acts at the time, stirred up by fear of the French enemy. Substitute Patriot Act for the Alien and Sedition Acts and Islam for French, and things suddenly don't seem quite so different from today.

Other provisions in the Alien and Sedition Acts proved equally constitutionally problematic, including granting judiciary power to the executive branch.

The Acts outraged many in Kentucky. Several counties in the Commonwealth adopted resolutions condemning the acts, including Fayette, Clark, Bourbon, Madison and Woodford. A Madison County Kentucky militia regiment issued an ominous resolution of its own, stating, "The Alien and Sedition Bills are an infringement of the Constitution and of natural rights, and that we cannot approve or submit to them."(7) Several thousand people gathered at an outdoor meeting protesting the acts in Lexington on August 13.

Jefferson penned the original draft of the Kentucky Resolutions within a month of Congress passing the Sedition Act. The Tenth Amendment served as the lynchpin in his reasoning.

> "That the several States composing, the United States of America, are not united on the principle of unlimited submission to their general government; but that, by a compact under the style and title of a Constitution for the United States, and of amendments thereto, they constituted a general government for special purposes — delegated to that government certain definite powers, reserving, each State to itself, the residuary mass of right to their own self-government; and that whensoever the general

> government assumes undelegated powers, its acts
> are unauthoritative, void, and of no force."

He repeated the Tenth Amendment verbatim three times in the resolutions.

After outlining each constitutional violation and overreach of federal power, Jefferson called for action – nullify now!

> "Therefore this commonwealth is determined, as it
> doubts not its co-States are, to submit to
> undelegated, and consequently unlimited powers in
> no man, or body of men on earth: that in cases of an
> abuse of the delegated powers, the members of the
> general government, being chosen by the people, a
> change by the people would be the constitutional
> remedy; but, where powers are assumed which have
> not been delegated, **a nullification of the act is the
> rightful remedy**: that every State has a natural right
> in cases not within the compact, (casus non fœderis)
> to nullify of their own authority all assumptions of
> power by others within their limits: that without this
> right, they would be under the dominion, absolute
> and unlimited, of whosoever might exercise this right
> of judgment for them."

Jefferson sent former Virginia ratifying convention delegate Wilson Cary Nicholas a draft of the resolution, likely hoping the state legislator could get them introduced in Virginia. In October, 1798, Wilson indicated that Kentucky state representative John Breckinridge was willing to introduce the resolutions in Kentucky. Breckinridge suffered from tuberculosis and made a recuperative trip to Sweet Springs, Va. late in August of that year. Nicholas likely gave the Kentucky lawmaker a copy of Jefferson's draft during that trip.

On Nov. 7, 1798, Gov. James Garrard addressed the Kentucky state legislature, noting the vehement opposition to the Alien and Sedition

Acts. He said Kentucky was, "if not in a state of insurrection, yet utterly disaffected to the federal government. And noted that the state "being deeply interested in the conduct of the national government, must have a right to applaud or to censure that government, when applause or censure becomes its due," urging the legislature to reaffirm its support of the U.S. Constitution while, "entering your protest against all unconstitutional laws and impolitic proceedings."(8)

That same day, Breckinridge announced to the House he intended to submit resolutions addressing Garrard's message. The following day, the Fayette County lawmaker followed through, introducing an amended version of Jefferson's draft. Most notably, Breckinridge omitted the word nullification from the actual version considered by the Kentucky legislature, seeking to moderate the tone of the resolution. Removal of the nullification reference apparently didn't bother Jefferson, and in fact, did little to change the fundamental thrust of the resolution. By declaring the Alien and Sedition Act unconstitutional, null and void, the Kentucky legislature voted on a nullification resolution, even with the actual word omitted.

The resolution passed the House on Nov. 10 with only three dissenting votes. The Senate unanimously concurred three days later, and Gov. Garrard signed the resolution on Nov. 16.

The following day, Jefferson sent a draft of his resolution to James Madison, writing, "We should distinctly affirm all the important principles they contain, so as to hold to that ground in the future, and leave the matter in such a train as that we may not be committed absolutely to push the matter to extremities, and yet may be free to push as far as events will render prudent."

John Taylor introduced Madison's resolution in the Virginia Assembly the following month. He described the resolutions, "as a rejection of the false choice between timidity and civil war." Taylor argued that state nullification provided an alternative to popular nullification – outright rebellion. In legislative debates, he argued that "the will of

11

the people was better expressed through organized bodies dependent on that will, than by tumultuous meetings; that thus the preservation of peace and good order would be more secure." (9) The Virginia Resolutions passed on Dec. 24, 1798.

The Kentucky and Virginia resolutions did not meet with resounding support. In fact, Federalist controlled northern states opposed the idea of nullification, several countering with official resolutions of their own. The Massachusetts legislature declared:

> *"But they deem it their duty solemnly to declare that, while they hold sacred the principle that consent of the people is the only pure source of just and legitimate power, they cannot admit the right of the state legislatures to denounce the administration of that government to which the people themselves, by a solemn compact, have exclusively committed their national concerns."*

Kentucky responded with a second resolution in 1799, notably including the word "nullification," omitted in the Kentucky Resolutions of 1798 passed by the state legislature.

> *"That this commonwealth considers the federal Union, upon the terms and for the purposes specified in the late compact, conducive to the liberty and happiness of the several states: That it does now unequivocally declare its attachment to the Union, and to that compact, agreeably to its obvious and real intention, and will be among the last to seek its dissolution: That, if those who administer the general government be permitted to transgress the limits fixed by that compact, by a total disregard to the special delegations of power therein contained, an annihilation of the state governments, and the creation, upon their ruins, of a general consolidated*

government, will be the inevitable consequence: That the principle and construction, contended for by sundry of the state legislatures, that the general government is the exclusive judge of the extent of the powers delegated to it, stop nothing short of despotism—since the discretion of those who administer the government, and not the Constitution, would be the measure of their powers: That the several states who formed that instrument, being sovereign and independent, have the unquestionable right to judge of its infraction; and, That a nullification, by those sovereignties, of all unauthorized acts done under color of that instrument, is the rightful remedy." (Emphasis added)

We cannot judge the validity of the Principles of '98 based on short-term political outcomes. A Republican assent to power, driven by popular opposition to the Alien and Sedition Acts and capped by Jefferson's presidential victory in the 1800 election, rendered the nullification issue moot, at least for the time being. But the staying power of the principles became evident just a few years later when the same northeastern lawmakers who condemned the Kentucky and Virginia resolutions invoked those very principles to fight Jefferson's embargo of 1807.

With both the British and French seizing American shipping bound for each other's ports, Jefferson chose to wage economic warfare, forbidding any U.S. merchant vessel to sail for any foreign port, anywhere in the world. Finding the usurpation shoe on the other foot, Massachusetts suddenly became an ardent supporter of a state's right to judge the constitutionality of an act, declaring the embargo, "in many respects unjust, oppressive and unconstitutional, and not legally binding on the citizens of this state."

And Connecticut Governor Jonathan Trumbull channeled James Madison.

> "Whenever our national legislature is led to overleap the prescribed bounds of their constitutional powers, on the State Legislatures, in great emergencies, devolves the arduous task – it is their right – it becomes their duty, to interpose their protecting shield between the right and liberty of the people, and the assumed power of the General Government." (10)

Over the next 50 years, numerous states advanced the Principles of '98, fighting against federal overreach on a wide range of issues, including federal conscription during the War of 1812. Daniel Webster of New Hampshire wrote, "The operation of measures thus unconstitutional and illegal ought to be prevented by a resort to other measures which are both constitutional and legal. It will be the solemn duty of the State governments to protect their own authority over their own militia, and to interpose between their citizens and arbitrary power. These are among the objects for which the State governments exist" (11)

Nullification was also invoked during the battle against the Second National Bank, against tariffs in the 1830s and to fight fugitive slave laws in the 1840s and 50s. In an argument against the bank, the Ohio legislature"recognized and approved" the Kentucky and Virginia Resolutions of 1798.

Members of every political party appealed to the Principles at various times, proving they are more than partisan tools used to advance specific agendas, or the property of one political wing.

Late in life, as political winds shifted, Madison seemingly backed away from nullification, going as far as to declare a lone state does not have the right to unilaterally nullify, at least not in the specific manner South Carolina concocted during the tariff crisis of the 1830s.

Opponents of nullification use this, along with other evidence, including the omission of the word nullification in the final draft of the Kentucky Resolution of 1798, and the complete absence of the word in the Virginia Resolutions, to declare the Principles of '98 fatally flawed. But despite rabid opposition to nullification by those favoring expanding federal power over the last 230 plus years, the Principles of '98 demonstrate amazing staying power. Why? Because the case for nullification rests not only on a couple of resolutions passed more than 200 years ago, but on the same philosophical bedrock as the Constitution itself – an understanding that the central government wields limited power constrained by checks and balances. The Kentucky and Virginia Resolutions lay out the principles of nullification and serve as an invaluable tool to understand the concepts. But we don't rely on the resolutions alone to defend the principle. In fact, nullification digs its roots into the very soil of the American system itself. It would remain a logical and valid option even if Jefferson and Madison never took quill to parchment. To properly understand the nature of America's Republican system is to embrace nullification. Despite his later apparent equivocation, Madison defends the idea in the strongest terms in the Report of 1800.

> *"If the deliberate exercise of dangerous powers, palpably withheld by the Constitution, could not justify the parties to it, in interposing even so far as to arrest the progress of the evil, and thereby to preserve the Constitution itself, as well as to provide for the safety of the parties to it, there would be an end to all relief from usurped power, and a direct subversion of the rights specified or recognized under all state constitutions, as well as a plain denial of the fundamental principle on which our independence itself was declared."*

St. George Tucker wrote the first extended, systematic commentary on the Constitution. Published in 1803, *View of the Constitution of the*

United States served as an important law book for the next 50 years. Tucker explained the nature of the government formed by the Constitution

> *"The government thus established may be*
> *pronounced to be a confederal republic, composed of*
> *several independent and sovereign democratic states,*
> *united for their common defense, and security against*
> *foreign nations, and for the purpose of harmony, and*
> *mutual intercourse between each other; each state*
> *retaining an entire liberty of exercising, as it thinks*
> *proper, all those parts of its sovereignty, which are*
> *not mentioned in the Constitution, or act of union, as*
> *parts that ought to be exercised in common."*
> *(Emphasis original) (12)*

The framers intended the states to serve as a check on federal power, and it logically follows that states should possess some mechanism to step in when Congress, the president or some ABC bureaucratic agency wields power it doesn't rightly possess. Nullification provides the means to that end.

Just say, "No."

We don't advocate nullification simply because Jefferson and Madison did. We advocate nullification because it stands as the rightful remedy when the federal government overreaches. It is not an act of extremism, nor an act of rebellion. And it certainly isn't "unconstitutional."

From elementary school, most Americans learn that Washington D.C. serves as the seat of power. All things flow down from the federal government. The Constitution contains a supremacy clause, doesn't it?

And therein lies the problem.

Most Americans balk at the idea of states saying, "No," to Fedzilla because they don't really understand who's in charge.

2

WHO'S THE BOSS?

In the 1975 classic *Monty Python and the Holy Grail*, King Arthur "rides" into town, passing by a mortician pushing a cart full of dead bodies collected in a medieval village. The mortician pauses to chat with a "customer" who just delivered a not quite dead victim to the cart.

"Who's that then?" the customer asks as Arthur "gallops" by.

"I don't know," the mortician replies.

"Must be a King."

"Why?"

"He hasn't got s#$% all over him."

We might chuckle at such a notion today, but the short dialogue illustrates political realities in much of the world throughout most of human history. Rulers reigned supreme. They enjoyed unlimited rights, power and authority. Rulers expected subjects to submit without exception, without question.

How did a king come to possess unlimited power?

By divine right.

In the following scene, Arthur's conversation with a peasant named Dennis and his female companion juxtaposes rule by divine right with the modern notion of government by consent.

After Arthur rides up behind Dennis and mistakes him for an old lady, Dennis challenges Arthur's condescending attitude.

"What I object to is you automatically treat me like an inferior."

Arthur defends himself, asserting his authority as King. This spurs Dennis to launch into a political diatribe. As the pair walk toward Dennis' female companion, slogging around on her hands and knees in some "lovely filth," the conversation continues until Arthur gets fed up and orders Dennis to shut up.

"Be quiet. I order you to be quiet!"

The woman isn't impressed

"Order, eh? Who does he think he is?"

"I am your king," Arthur proclaims, obviously expecting that fact to end the conversation.

"Well, I didn't vote for you," the woman replies matter-of-factly.

"You don't vote for kings," Arthur retorts incredulously.

"Well how'd you become king then?"

With angelic music playing in the background, Arthur explains his divine right to rule.

"The Lady of the Lake, her arm clad in the purest shimmering samite, held aloft Excalibur from the bosom of the water, signifying by divine providence that I, Arthur, was to carry Excalibur. THAT is why I am your king."

Dennis interjects. "Listen, strange women lyin' in ponds distributin' swords is no basis for a system of government. Supreme executive power derives from a mandate from the masses, not from some farcical aquatic ceremony."

Many elected officials and bureaucrats today still act as if they hold power by some mystical divine right. True, they don't claim authority based upon royal lineage, heavenly appointment, or "just because some watery tart threw a sword at them." But they do govern with a certain air of superiority. In the United States, attending the right universities, membership in approved organizations and the prerequisite family connections, along with anointment from the proper media outlets, serve as a secularized version of the idea of divine right.

In short, many politicians think they know better than you do how to run your life.

"So shut up and let us do our job, you bloody peasants!"

Oh, our public servants usually say the right words, commiserating with the masses, creating the impression that they are "one of us." They know how to play to the hoi polloi. They go hunting with constituents, join laborers on assembly lines, and show up at town hall meetings sporting blue jeans and plaid shirts – making sure, of course, the cameras roll the entire time.

But every once in a while, in unguarded moments, true feelings slip out.

> "You go into these small towns in Pennsylvania and,
> like a lot of small towns in the Midwest, the jobs have
> been gone now for 25 years and nothing's replaced

them," Pres. Barack Obama said on the campaign trail
in 2008. "And they fell through the Clinton
Administration, and the Bush Administration, and
each successive administration has said that
somehow these communities are gonna regenerate
and they have not. And it's not surprising then they
get bitter, they cling to guns or religion or antipathy
to people who aren't like them or anti-immigrant
sentiment or anti-trade sentiment as a way to explain
their frustrations."(1)

Ah, those poor peasants, toting their guns and bitterly clinging to
their mythical religion in order to cope with the complex world.

Or how about Sen. John Kerry? He knows how to spend your money.
And anyway, you can't be trusted to do the right thing with it.

"A tax cut is non-targeted. If you put a tax cut into the
hands of either a business or an individual today,
there is no guarantee they're gonna invest their
money. There's no guarantee they're gonna invest
their money in the United States. They're free to go
to invest anywhere that they want, if they choose to
invest... The fact is; none of those people are
guaranteed to invest that money in any of the new
projects that we are... So government, yes
government, has the ability to make a decision that
the private sector won't necessarily make today."(2)

And when a reporter asked Rep. Nancy Pelosi to cite the
constitutional authorization for health insurance mandates, she
revealed her disdain for constitutional restraints.

"Are you serious? Are you serious?"(3)

Condescension isn't just a Democratic phenomenon, during the
health care debate, Kansas Rep. Lynn Jenkins suggested, "People

should be given the opportunity to take care of themselves with a refund, or an advanceable [sic] tax credit, to go be a grown-up and go buy the insurance."(4)

Many government servants seem to suffer from an overinflated view of their own intelligence, education and pedigree. As a result, they think they can conjure up solutions to virtually any problem. But only if those pesky commoners will just get out of the way and let them do their jobs. This becomes particularly apparent when it comes to economic policy. Amazingly, elected politicians and appointed bureaucrats think they can "manage" millions of people freely entering into voluntary exchanges. One need only look at the havoc wreaked by central planners in the economy of the Soviet Union to see the fallacy of this notion. Yet "policymakers" push ahead undeterred, trying to micromanage every aspect of economic life.

And these politicians tend to view their election to office as a sort of divine right to rule and impose their prerogative on constituents, regardless of what the general population thinks, wants or believes.

"We know best."

This certainly is not a new phenomenon. French economist and political philosopher Frederic Bastiat railed against political writers of his day. The political elite clung to this misguided notion in 1850 too.

> "In fact, these writers on public affairs begin by supposing that people have within themselves no means of discernment; no motivation to action. The writers assume that people are inert matter, passive particles, motionless atoms, at best a kind of vegetation indifferent to its own manner of existence. They assume that people are susceptible to being shaped – by the will and hand of another person – into an infinite variety of forms, more or less symmetrical, artistic and perfected.

"Moreover, not one of these writers on governmental affairs hesitates to imagine that he himself – under the title of organizer, discoverer, legislator, or founder – is this will and hand, this universal motivating force, this creative power whose sublime mission is to mold these scattered materials – persons – into a society.

"These socialist writers look upon people in the same manner that the gardener views his trees. Just as the gardener capriciously shapes the trees into pyramids, parasols, cubes, vases, fans and other forms, just so does the socialist writer whimsically shape human beings into groups, series, centers, sub-centers, honeycombs, labor corps and other variations. And just as the gardener needs axes, pruning hooks, saws, and shears to shape his trees, just so does the socialist writer need the force that he can find only in law to shape human beings."(5)

The 2008 economic crisis vividly illustrated the very real divide between the American people and those who hold office. Polling at the time showed Americans opposed the government bailout plan to buy "toxic" bank assets by three or four to one. But Republicans and Democrats, from Pres. G.W. Bush to candidate Barack Obama, came together in lock-step agreement with nearly unanimous support from mainstream media. Congress overwhelmingly passed the bailout bill.

And the Tea Party was born.

Writer Angelo M. Codevilla, observing the complete disregard of the people's wishes by those in power dubbed them "America's ruling class," in a July 2010 American Spectator article. He used the term not only to describe politicians, but the academic and media support system surrounding them.

"When this majority discovered that virtually no one in a position of power in either party or with a national voice would take their objections seriously, that decisions about their money were being made in bipartisan backroom deals with interested parties, and that the laws on these matters were being voted by people who had not read them, the term "political class" came into use. Then, after those in power changed their plans from buying toxic assets to buying up equity in banks and major industries but refused to explain why, when they reasserted *their right to decide ad hoc* on these and so many other matters, supposing them to be beyond the general public's understanding, the American people started referring to those in and around government as the "ruling class." And in fact Republican and Democratic office holders and their retinues show a similar presumption to dominate and fewer differences in tastes, habits, opinions, and sources of income among one another than between both and the rest of the country. They think, look, and act as a class."(6)

And this class believes it alone possess the smarts, know-how and foresight to rule.

A modern, secular divine right.

This all leads to a very important question.

Who's really the boss?

Simple answer: I am.

And you are.

When it comes right down to it, nobody can make you do anything, unless you let them. You've heard the old saying, "nothing is certain in life but death and taxes." And really, taxes don't count as a given either. Sure, the government can probably apply enough force to squeeze every last dime out of your wallet. But at the core, you still make the choice. You judge the cost of fighting the IRS too great and go ahead and send that check. But ultimately, you could accept the consequences and never pay a dime.

During the 17th and 18th centuries, theologians and philosophers began to recognize this reality and the idea of divine right slowly gave way to an understanding that each individual stands as a free moral agent. Nobody has an innate right to rule over another person. After all, if the God of the universe refuses to force humankind to submit to His will, how can a mere man justify forcing his will on the rest of humanity? John Locke rested his whole understanding of political power on this foundation.

> "To understand political power right, and derive it from its original, we must consider what state all men are naturally in, and that is, a state of perfect freedom to order their actions, and dispose of their possessions and persons as they think fit, within the bounds of the law of nature, without asking leave, or depending upon the will of any other man.
>
> "A state also of equality, wherein all the power and jurisdiction is reciprocal, no one having more than another: there being nothing more evident than that creatures of the same species and rank promiscuously born to all the same advantages of nature and the use of the same faculties, should also be equal one amongst another without subordination or subjection, unless the Lord and Master of them all should, by any manifest declaration of his will, set one above another and confer on him by an evident and clear appointment an undoubted right to dominion and sovereignty." (7)

The founders of the United States brought this idea with them, and it forms the cornerstone of the American experiment. Thomas Jefferson enshrined the concept in the opening words of the Declaration of Independence.

> "We hold these truths to be self-evident, **that all men are created equal**, that they are endowed by their Creator with certain unalienable Rights, that among these are Life, Liberty, and the Pursuit of Happiness." *(Emphasis added)*

Equality, as Locke and Jefferson use the term, doesn't literally mean sameness. Watch me swing a baseball bat and it quickly becomes evident that I am not equal to Manny Ramirez, at least not on the baseball diamond. On the other hand, it would probably prove pretty amusing to put Manny in a room full of professors talking quantum physics.

Clearly, we don't stand equal to one another in ability or outcome. Manny can swing a bat. Carrie Underwood can sing. Barack Obama can deliver a speech. Bill Gates can run a computer company. I can stop a hockey puck or two. And these innate differences create other inequalities. Just compare my bank account with Mr. Gates.

Progressives focus on these kinds of inequalities and seek government power to eliminate them. But they completely miss Jefferson's point. He was not talking about equality of abilities, or even equality of opportunity and outcomes. He referred to a more fundamental principle, that every human being has a natural right to determine her or his own path through life, and no other person possesses any inherent right to lord or rule over another. Manny can't make me his slave simply because he can slam a 90 mph fastball out of the park. Despite his superiority on the baseball diamond, Ramirez doesn't enjoy all-encompassing superiority over me. Nor does anybody else on earth.

"All men are created equal."

I'm the boss of me.

Eighteenth century American legal scholar St. George Tucker put it this way.

> "By equality, in a democracy, is to be understood, equality of civil rights, and not of condition. Equality of rights necessarily produces inequality of possessions; because, by the laws of nature and of equality, every man has a right to use his faculties in an honest way, and the fruits of his labor, thus acquired, are his own. But some men have more strength than others; some more health; some more industry; and some more skill and ingenuity, than others; and according to these, and other circumstances the products of their labor must be various, and their property must become unequal." *(8)*

In an attempt to create a utopian society without these inherent inequalities, big-government progressives actually trample the very idea of equality upon which the United States was founded. They set themselves up above others as rulers by their own grant of divine right. It flows out of a sense of self-righteousness. They view their ends as good. And perhaps they are. Eliminate injustice in the world. Protect the environment. Heal the sick. Who can really disagree? Lofty goals indeed. But in their haste to achieve good – the "ruling class" forgets that I'm the boss. And no matter how wonderful their vision, they have no right to force me to take any action to achieve their ends.

But if each individual gets to play the role of boss, how can we ever get anything done as a society? Most people recognize the necessity of working together for mutual benefit. From economics to defense to the natural human desire for fellowship, we need each other. Sixteenth century political philosopher Johannes Althusius recognized this need for association.

"Truly, in living this life no man is self-sufficient, or adequately endowed by nature...Necessity therefore induces associations; and the want to things necessary for life, which are acquired and communicated by the help and aid of one's associates, conserves it. For this reason, it is evident that the commonwealth, or civil society, exists by nature, and that man is by nature is a civil animal who strives eagerly for association."(9)

Locke also acknowledged the human need and desire to group together in civil society.

"God having made man such a creature, that in his own judgment it was not good for him to be alone, put him under strong obligations of necessity, convenience and inclination, to drive him into society, as well as fitted him with understanding and language to continue and enjoy it."(10)

Of course, we all know that if you stick two people in a room together, they will quickly find a way to disagree. A cartoon features two aliens talking to each other, one holding a "human farm," reminiscent of the ant farms we played with as kids. The second holds a stack of boxes, each labeled with a different Christian denomination – Catholic, Baptist, Presbyterian, Lutheran, etc. He says to his friend, "Careful that you don't mix them. They will fight. Then again, even if you don't mix them, they will subdivide and fight anyway."

Face it; we can muster up infinite ways to create conflict. Somehow, we have to figure out a way to work with each other. In order to live together and cooperate for our common good, we have to come up with some agreed upon common rules to live by and unbiased judges to settle disputes. We need a mechanism to protect our property, which Locke broadly defined as life, liberty and estate.(11) Without some structure in place, society will quickly devolve into power struggles and outright warfare, no better than the state of nature we all exist in to begin with.

To deal with this reality, we institute and empower government.

Self-ownership serves as the starting point. From there, it logically follows that government can only legitimately derive its power from consent.

Jefferson started with this idea when framing the Declaration of Independence.

"That to secure these rights, Governments are instituted among Men, deriving their just powers from the consent of the governed."

In order to live peacefully together and to better facilitate protecting our lives, liberty and property; we delegate certain powers to a government. Locke describes the process of forming government in his Second Treatises.

> "Men being, as has been said, by nature all free, equal and independent, no one can be put out of this estate, and subject to the political power of another, without his own consent. The only way whereby anyone divests himself of his natural liberty and puts on the bonds of civil society, is by agreeing with other men to join and unite into a community, for their comfortable, safe and peaceable living one amongst another, in a secure enjoyment of their properties, and a greater security against any that are not of it."*(12)*

It logically follows that an individual delegating power retains the right to take that authority away.

Thus, the people always remain sovereign.

I'm the boss.

To understand nullification, one must always keep in mind the ultimate source of authority. It doesn't flow from the president. Not Congress. Not the Supreme Court. Not the U.N.

So, who wields supreme authority?

You do.

I do.

We all do.

Many object to the idea of nullification because they understand it as an act of rebellion against authority. But when you understand who actually holds power, nullifiers exercise legitimate authority, restraining a rebellious government wielding power beyond what was given. Government only maintains legitimacy when it remains constrained within the parameters the people set. In the United States, the Constitution defines those governmental limits. When the feds exercise powers not delegated to them by the Constitution, they act without authority, and nullification – saying, "No, we will not submit to this act," - becomes the rightful remedy. According to Locke, when a government acts against the people, or asserts itself outside of its constitutional bounds, it puts itself into a state of war against the people.(13) At that point, any obligation of obedience to government dissolves.

When you understand who stands sovereign and how grants of power flow, the principle behind nullification crystalizes. Instead of perceiving it as a rebellious act of defiance against the supreme power in Washington D.C., you will see it for what it really is – a mechanism checking power that the people delegated to the federal government in the first place.

Sovereign people create governments through written constitutions. In essence, a constitution serves as contract between the people (the principal) and the governments they create (the agent). Constitutions establish the parameters within which government must operate.

Through constitutions, the people set limits and constrain government to specific powers and roles. As the sovereign, "We the People" of the United States delegated certain powers to government, first to the states, and later to the federal government through those states. The federal government may not legally act outside of those enumerated powers.

The American system is amazing. The framers envisioned a Republic, creating a network of checks and balances facilitating political society, protecting property and providing for a common defense; all the while restraining governmental power and protecting the rights of the individual.

But for the system to work, we must abide by the rules.

3

RULES WERE MADE TO BE FOLLOWED

The final game of the season. Stands awash with sounds and color. Drums beat rhythmically. Horns blast. Fans chant in unison as the referee places the ball in the lush green grass and the teams line up face to face, preparing for one more epic battle.

The visitors trail 21-14 as the final seconds tick off the clock. It's fourth-and-goal at the 1-yard line. The quarterback takes his place under center as a deafening roar rises up from the partisan home crowd. The quarterback takes the snap, turns and smacks the ball into the running back's gut. The halfback plunges forward, legs churning for the end zone. He looks left, darts right and leaps toward the goal line. A mighty collision, as a 240-pound linebacker meets him mid-air. The impact throws the ball carrier backward, and he tumbles to the ground a half yard short of the end zone. After a moment of silence, the home fans erupt in jubilation as the horn sounds ending the game.

But wait.

A sudden movement draws the crowd's attention toward the referee. He runs along the goal line, both arms raised high in the air, signaling a touchdown. The fans groan in displeasure. Home players stand stunned. The coach goes apoplectic on the sideline. The running back clearly crashed to the turf well short of a touchdown.

Several minutes pass as officials huddle closely together in consultation. One steps under the hood to review the instant replay. Moments later, as he walks to center field, the crowd falls nearly silent. Then the referee keys his mic and offers an explanation.

"Even though the runner was down short of the end zone, we feel he was close enough to warrant granting him the touchdown. We believe it is in the best interest of the fans, and of the league in general, for this game to continue into overtime. The rules reserve certain interpretive latitude to officials. The running back's effort certainly deserves a reward. The touchdown stands."

A ridiculous scenario, you say? The referee can't arbitrarily ignore the rules of the game, even if it is for the "better," you argue?

Indeed.

We all intuitively understand – we need rules. And we must follow them.

The U.S. Constitution provides a framework, the rulebook, if you will, for the federal government; each clause, each principle, carefully crafted for a specific reason. Virtually the entire document aims to define, constrain and control federal power. When we begin to ignore and rewrite various checks and balances written into the Constitution by the framers, we tear at the very fabric of the Republic. And we run the risk of unleashing a torrent of power that will soon wash away the freedoms and liberties the founders cherished.

Thomas Jefferson said, "The two enemies of the people are criminals and government, so let us tie the second down with the chains of the Constitution so the second will not become the legalized version of the first."

A football game would degenerate into chaos without set rules and adherence to them. If referees arbitrarily awarded touchdowns, the game would cease to have any real meaning. Can you imagine the ridicule that would pour down on an NFL official claiming to have unlimited power to make up rules on the field, regardless of the rulebook?

Althusius wrote, "All power is limited by definite boundaries and laws. No power is absolute, indefinite, arbitrary and lawless. Every power is bound to laws, right and equity."(1)

Yet many Americans act as if the president, the Congress, or the Supreme Court possesses unlimited power. They may express frustration with unconstitutional overreach, but ultimately, they shrug and accept it. "The Supreme Court ruled, so that's just how it is," they argue. Pundits and average citizens alike react in horror at the mere suggestion that state governments should defy a court ruling, ignore a presidential executive order or nullify an unconstitutional act.

Most Americans, at least tacitly, accept the idea that the federal government wields unlimited, absolute, supreme power- a sort of national political football game not bound by any rules.

The founders never intended such a thing.

Delegation of Power

A referee's authority to officiate an NFL football game flows from the league. When a candidate meets the criteria set by the NFL, league officials authorize him to don the striped shirt and referee games. He must call the contest according to the rules set by the NFL, rules enumerated in the official rulebook. He can't just make up rules as he goes. And he can't willy-nilly insert his own interpretation of the regulations. The referee must call the game according to set and established criteria. He enjoys a delegation of power from the league, but he must exercise it within its prescribed limits. No calling touchdowns because he decides it will make the game more exciting, or because he wants to inject his sense of fairness into the contest.

And it is self-evident that if the NFL hired me to referee football, it wouldn't give me the authority to umpire a Major League Baseball game, referee an NHL hockey game or arrest a drunk driver. An NFL ref's authority extends only to a limited arena - the NFL football field.

The NFL official operates within a delegation of power from the league. The referee, in essence, serves as an agent. The league acts as the sovereign. A sovereign can always revoke delegated power. The NFL can revoke the ref's authority at any time. It can change the rulebook or demand the ref adhere to a given interpretation of the rule. It can even dissolve the league. The referee enjoys no such authority or prerogative. He merely wields the power given to him – he simply refs the game.

The NFL is boss.

In the same way, a government serves as an agent of the people. The people delegate government specific, defined powers. And as we've already discussed, the people remain sovereign. The people can revoke a delegation of power at any time. They can even dissolve the government and start over, as the American colonists did in 1776 when they severed political ties with England.

> *"That whenever any Form of Government becomes destructive of these ends, it is the Right of the People to alter or to abolish it, and to institute new Government, laying its foundation on such principles and organizing its powers in such form, as to them shall seem most likely to effect their Safety and Happiness."* – Declaration of Independence

You and I are the bosses.

Legitimate government must follow the rules – the Constitution. And any power exercised by the federal government beyond those delegated is, by definition, void and of no effect.

Historians generally consider Alexander Hamilton the framer most sympathetic to a strong, national government. Yet even he emphatically argued that the Constitution strictly limited the power of the general government. In Federalist 78, Hamilton wrote:

> *"There is no position which depends on clearer principles, than that every act of a delegated authority, contrary to the tenor of the commission under which it is exercised, is void. No legislative act, therefore, contrary to the Constitution, can be valid. To deny this, would be to affirm, that the deputy is greater than his principal; that the servant is above his master; that the representatives of the people are superior to the people themselves; that men acting by virtue of powers, may do not only what their powers do not authorize, but what they forbid."*

A constitution is nothing but a legal document whereby a sovereign delegates certain powers to a government. Have you ever stopped to think about why the opening words of the U.S. Constitution, **We the People** appear in large, ornate letters? When an 18th century British king issued a grant, his name always appeared at the top in the same fashion. The framers merely replaced the king's name with "We the People," signifying the sovereign authority from which the delegation of power flowed.(2)

The people.

You and I.

The bosses.

The Constitution defines and limits the power of the federal government in the same way the NFL rulebook defines and limits the role of the NFL ref, or a contract with your bank defines and limits the terms of your mortgage. Article I, Sec. 8 lists the powers of Congress. The framers considered it obvious that listing powers excluded any not on the list. Alexander Hamilton makes this clear in Federalist 83.

> *"This specification of particulars [the 18 enumerated powers of Article I, Section 8] evidently excludes all pretension to a general legislative authority, because an affirmative grant of special powers would be absurd as well as useless if a general authority was intended."*

Virginia ratification convention delegate Richard Henry Lee made the same argument during the ratification debates.

> *"It goes on the principle that all power is in the people, and that rulers have no powers but what are enumerated in that paper. When a question arises with respect to the legality of any power, exercised or assumed by Congress, it is plain on the side of the governed. Is it enumerated in the Constitution? If it be, it is legal and just. It is otherwise arbitrary and unconstitutional."(3)*

But many in the ratifying conventions were not satisfied with this implicit understanding. They wanted an explicit statement defining the limits of federal authority. And the Tenth Amendment was born.

The powers not delegated to the United States by the Constitution, nor prohibited by it to the States, are reserved to the States respectively, or to the people.

Any power and authority not delegated to the federal government remains exactly where it was prior to the ratification of the Constitution – with the states and the people.

The ratifying documents issued by the states agreeing to the Constitution reveal how the people understood the form of government they were approving. The Virginia ratifying instrument makes it clear that the citizens of the Commonwealth had no intention of giving up any powers other than those specifically delegated to the general government.

> *"We the Delegates of the People of Virginia duly elected in pursuance of a recommendation from the General Assembly and now met in Convention having fully and freely investigated and discussed the proceedings of the Federal Convention and being prepared as well as the most mature deliberation hath enabled us to decide thereon Do in the name and in behalf of the People of Virginia* **declare and make known that the powers granted under the Constitution being derived from the People of the United States may be resumed by them whensoever the same shall be perverted to their injury or oppression and that every power not granted thereby remains with them and at their will:** *that therefore no right of any denomination can be cancelled abridged restrained or modified by the Congress by the Senate or House of Representatives acting in any Capacity by the President or any Department or Officer of the United States except in those instances in which power is given by the Constitution for those purposes."* (Emphasis added)

Notice an important point, often overlooked. The Virginia ratifiers claimed the right to "resume" the powers delegated. In other words, if the federal government abused the authority granted, the people of Virginia reserved the right to take those powers back.

Virginia Governor Edmund Randolph served as a delegate at the Philadelphia Convention of 1787. He initially favored a stronger central government due to his frustrations with the limits of the Articles of Confederation. But he ultimately refused to sign the final draft of the Constitution, arguing that some sections remained too vague. Once he returned to Virginia, he switched course, becoming a supporter of ratification, arguing that the alternative – disunion - was unacceptable. He represented the middle ground between ardent Federalists, such as Madison, on the one hand, and vehement Anti-Federalists, such as Patrick Henry, on the other. Randolph ultimately helped broker the Old Dominion ratifying convention, promising the ratification instrument would enforce a limited view of federal power and also committing to the adoption of amendments after ratification. He, along with George Nicholas, who most considered something of a spokesman for Madison, swayed enough fence sitters to vote for ratification. This didn't simply represent some meaningless opinion offered by some rubes in Virginia. The legal rules of construction for a compact, or contract, dictate that when one party makes a stipulation to the agreement, that stipulation becomes binding upon all other parties to the compact. In other words, Virginia's ratifying instrument represents a part of the legal framework of the Constitution itself.

Nicholas made this point in a speech during the ratification convention.

> "The Constitution cannot be binding upon Virginia, but with these conditions," he said. "If 13 individuals are about to make a contract and one agrees to it, but at the same time declares that he understands its meaning, signification and intent, to be, what the words of the contract plainly and obviously denote, that it is not to be construed so as to impose any supplementary conditions upon him, and that he is to be exonerated from it, whensoever any such imposition shall be attempted – I ask whether in this case, these conditions on which he assented to it, would not be binding on the other 12? In like manner, these conditions will be binding on Congress. They can

*exercise no power that is not expressly granted
them."(4)*

Think of it like this. A friend comes to you with a business proposal, offering to bring you into a partnership with two other people. You look it over and decide the scheme looks pretty good, except you want to make it clear that your 25 percent cut of the profit will be calculated pre-tax. You write up a document accepting the partnership proposal, stipulating the pre-tax profit calculation method. If the group takes you on as a partner based on the terms in your acceptance document, it would obviously bind all them to the pre-tax profit calculation.

In the same way, Virginia entered into the union based on its ratifying instrument. The fact that the other states accepted its ratification and admitted it into the Union bound them to Virginia's expressed understanding of the constitution's meaning. So the foundation underlying the Principles of '98 didn't actually originate with Jefferson and Madison, but with Randolph, a Federalist.

During the latter days of the ratification debates, Randolph gave the following explanation.

> "Gentlemen will perhaps ask me, why, if you know the Constitution to be ambiguous, will you vote for it? I answer that I see a power, which will be probably exercised, to remedy this defect. The stile (5) of the ratification will remove this mischief. I do not ask for this concession – that human nature is just and absolutely honest. But I am fair when I say, that the nature of man is capable of virtue, where there is even a temptation, and that the defects in this system will be removed.
>
> "If it be not considered too early, as ratification has not yet been spoken of, I beg leave to speak of it. If I did believe, with the Honorable Gentleman, that all

*power not expressly retained was given up by the
people, I would detest this Government. But I never
thought so, nor do I now. If in the ratification we put
words to this purpose, - that all authority not given is
retained by the people, and may be resumed when
perverted to their oppression; and that no right can
be cancelled, abridged, or restrained, by the Congress,
or any officer of the United Sates; I say, if we do this, I
conceive that, as the stile of ratification would
manifest the principles on which Virginia adopted it,
we should be at liberty to consider as a violation of
the Constitution, every exercise of power not
expressly delegated therein. – I see no objection to
this. It is demonstrably clear to me, that rights not
given are retained, and that liberty of religion, and
other rights are secure."* (6)

Virginia was not the only state to include such restrictive language in
its ratification instrument. New York's document contains the
following clause.

*"That the Powers of Government may be reassumed
by the People, whensoever it shall become necessary
to their Happiness; that every Power, Jurisdiction and
right, which is not by the said Constitution clearly
delegated to the Congress of the United States, or the
departments of the Government thereof, remains to
the People of the several States, or to their respective
State Governments to whom they may have granted
the same; And that those Clauses in the said
Constitution, which declare, that Congress shall not
have or exercise certain Powers, do not imply that
Congress is entitled to any Powers not given by the
said Constitution; but such Clauses are to be
construed either as exceptions to certain specified
Powers, or as inserted merely for greater Caution."*

South Carolina ratifiers simply asserted, *"This Convention doth also declare, that no section or paragraph of the said Constitution warrants a construction that the states do not retain every power not expressly relinquished by them, and vested in the general government of the Union."*

So, a definite flow of power exists. Americans initially delegated political authority to their state governments. Later, through the states, "We the People" gave limited powers to the federal government through the Constitution. The people always remain sovereign. The states retain powers delegated to them through the people – sovereign within their own realm, while the federal government maintains authority to act within its prescribed role. In other words, the people and the states do not give up their ability to make decisions within their own sphere simply because they choose to associate with another body - the federal government.

Madison explained the division of powers in Federalist 39.

> *"The local or municipal authorities form distinct and independent portions of the supremacy, no more subject, within their respective spheres, to the general authority than the general authority is subject to them, within its own sphere."*

In essence, the people transferred a few powers out of the "pot of power" already delegated to the state governments, and delegated them to the federal government. Representatives of the several states drafted the Constitution in order to delegate a few powers, up until then held exclusively by the states, to the new federal government. All powers not delegated were reserved to the states and the people, the state of things existing prior to ratification. And note the language of the Virginia ratifying instrument. The people (and by logic the states) reserved the right to take back those powers if the feds "perverted" them to oppress the people.

Most Americans have it completely backward. They think the federal government holds a higher position than the state governments, which stand above the people.

Nope.

People >State > fed

Many Americans don't realize that the original 13 colonies were actually considered independent sovereign nations prior to the ratification of the Constitution. In the Treaty of Paris, ending the American Revolution, the King of England recognized, "the said United States, viz., New Hampshire, Massachusetts Bay, Rhode Island and Providence Plantations, Connecticut, New York, New Jersey, Pennsylvania, Maryland, Virginia, North Carolina, South Carolina and Georgia, to be free sovereign and independent states, that he treats with them as such, and for himself, his heirs, and successors, relinquishes all claims to the government, propriety, and territorial rights of the same and every part thereof."

Later, through the authority already delegated by the sovereign people, the sovereign states came together as "parties to the compact" and created a federal system. The states preceded the union, and in fact, created it. A marriage doesn't spawn a bride and groom. A bride and groom join together to form a marriage – a union. And when two people get married, their union does not erase their individual character. They don't become one indistinguishable blob.

Article VII established that, "The Ratification of the Conventions of nine States, shall be sufficient for the Establishment of this Constitution between the States so ratifying the Same." But the creation of the union did not bind any non-ratifying state to it, even at the point those states ratifying included a majority of America's population. When the U.S. Congress first convened under the current Constitution, North Carolina and Rhode Island were not represented. In fact, Rhode Island did not join the union for over one year, and remained a sovereign nation up until it ratified on May 29, 1790. Need proof? North Carolina and Rhode Island sent no representatives or Senators to Congress until ratification was finalized in those two states.

This dismantles the notion advanced by many progressives insisting that the framers intended a single national government created by

43

the consent of a plurality of Americans. If that was true, North Carolina and Rhode Island would have automatically been bound to the Union, because at that point, far more than two-thirds of the American people were represented by ratifying states.

In fact, the so-called Anti-Federalists, who opposed the Constitution, feared that the federal government would become exactly what modern progressives claim it is: a single national government ruling over the states. Madison set about allaying this fear in Federalist 39.

> *"First. In order to ascertain the real character of the government, it may be considered in relation to the foundation on which it is to be established; to the sources from which its ordinary powers are to be drawn; to the operation of those powers; to the extent of them; and to the authority by which future changes in the government are to be introduced.*
>
> *"On examining the first relation, it appears, on one hand, that the Constitution is to be founded on the assent and ratification of the people of America, given by deputies elected for the special purpose; but, on the other, **that this assent and ratification is to be given by the people, not as individuals composing one entire nation, but as composing the distinct and independent States to which they respectively belong. It is to be the assent and ratification of the several States, derived from the supreme authority in each State, the authority of the people themselves. The act, therefore, establishing the Constitution, will not be a national, but a federal act.***
>
> *"That it will be a federal and not a national act, as these terms are understood by the objectors; the act of the people, as forming so many independent States, not as forming one aggregate nation, is obvious from this single consideration, that it is to result neither from the decision of a majority of the people of the Union, nor from that of a majority of the States. It must result from the unanimous assent*

of the several States that are parties to it, differing no otherwise from their ordinary assent than in its being expressed, not by the legislative authority, but by that of the people themselves. Were the people regarded in this transaction as forming one nation, the will of the majority of the whole people of the United States would bind the minority, in the same manner as the majority in each State must bind the minority; and the will of the majority must be determined either by a comparison of the individual votes, or by considering the will of the majority of the States as evidence of the will of a majority of the people of the United States. Neither of these rules have been adopted. **Each State, in ratifying the Constitution, is considered as a sovereign body, independent of all others, and only to be bound by its own voluntary act.** *In this relation, then, the new Constitution will, if established, be a federal, and not a national constitution."* (Emphasis added)

To understand the nature of the Constitution, we must keep in mind the proper flow of power from the people to the states to the federal government. It then becomes clear that the Constitution serves as a contract, with an agent - the federal government - assigned specific powers and responsibilities from the people. Jefferson and Madison called it a compact. And like any contract, we must interpret it by looking at its original meaning, purposes and context. To do otherwise, turns the Constitution into something completely different.

Words mean things.

And context illuminates meaning.

Context not only includes other words and articles in the Constitution, but also what the framers and ratifiers wrote and said about it. Supporters of the Constitution worked hard to "sell" the document to skeptical state conventions and the American people at large. Their words illuminate exactly what the ratifiers believed they were agreeing to. As we have seen, the Constitution was sold as a limited delegation of power to the federal government with all other powers remaining with the states and the people.

But Progressives view the Constitution as a living, breathing document. Barack Obama wrote in *The Audacity of Hope*:

"Ultimately, though, I have to side with Justice Breyer's view of the Constitution—that it is not a static but rather a living document, and must be read in the context of an ever-changing world."

In other words, according to the progressive world-view, the Constitution means – whatever they want it to mean. Their reasoning holds that in this ever-changing world we can't possibly know what the founders would think about things like freedom of speech in the Internet age, search and seizure in an era of wireless wiretapping or health insurance in our high-tech society. The world changes, thus context changes. So, they decide what the Constitution means and apply it as they see fit.

Bunk!

The framers included an amendment process to in order to adapt the Constitution to a changing world. They never intended for politicians to play fast and loose with the language of the document to make it mean what they want it to mean in the name of "adaptation."

The Constitution provides clear, specific instructions establishing and defining the U.S. system of government. The House of Representatives originates spending. The federal government shall not abridge freedom of speech, press or religion. The president must be at least 35-years-old and a citizen of the U.S. Clear and straight-forward.

But it goes deeper than that. The document's framers built upon the philosophical foundation – a philosophical foundation promoting individual liberty, respect for private property and a general distrust of concentrated power. We know this because the founders wrote volumes outlining their philosophies and ideas. We know this because we can study notes from the ratification debates and read the arguments of opponents. We know this because we can study John

Locke, and other philosophers who informed the thinking of the founders. We know this because we can pick up a copy of the Federalist Papers and read exactly how supporters sold the structure of the Republic to the people of the states.

Context does not change. It remains static, as much a part of the document as the words themselves. The philosophical framework undergirding the Constitution remains unchanged. And basic human nature does not change. People are no different today than they were in the 1780s. Power still corrupts and those charged with exercising authority still need fences to hem them in.

We live in the same world the framers lived in. We just play with more sophisticated toys.

So, to proclaim the Constitution living and breathing – deviating from the clear meaning the founders intended – rejects the very philosophy holding the document together. To advance their ideas, progressives must make the Constitution liquid, molding into a form that fits their needs. Manipulating it through the courts. Divorcing the Constitution from its underlying philosophical framework. Rendering it utterly meaningless.

That's exactly what has happened over the last 100 years or more. Progressive thought slowly but surely transformed the Constitution and the nature of the federal government. Instead of possessing limited powers for specific purposes, we now face a monstrosity with virtually unlimited power to do anything it pleases.

During a radio interview discussing the federal health care act, the host asked Kentucky Rep. John Yarmuth, "What can't the federal government do if it can mandate citizens to buy a product?"

His answer speaks volumes.

"It really doesn't prohibit the government from doing virtually anything – the federal government. So I don't know the answer to your question, because I am not sure there is anything under current interpretation of the commerce clause that the government couldn't do."

Can anybody argue with a straight face that the founders intended to create a central government vested with unlimited powers? Wasn't that precisely what Americans fought a bloody Revolutionary War to escape from? Clearly, something is wrong with this picture.

Before we can talk about state nullification of unconstitutional acts, we first must agree on what exactly the Constitution means. We have to agree upon a mode of interpretation that makes sense and remains true to the intent of the framers and ratifiers.

The answer lies in originalism.

4

IT MEANS WHAT IT MEANS.

"Get your facts first, then you can distort them as you please." – Mark Twain

Before considering the practical application of nullification, we must first come to some basic agreement as to what exactly the Constitution means. Nullification is not, after all, a way for states to simply ignore laws they don't happen to like. States may only legitimately nullify, "palpable and alarming" infractions of the Constitution.

In the game of Chess, each piece has its own particular mode of movement. For instance, the rules stipulate that a king may move one square in any direction. On the other hand, a bishop may move any number of squares diagonally, but cannot jump over other pieces. A rook can move any number of squares forward, backward or to either side. The rules of the game constrain each piece to its specific powers. A king can't willy-nilly move two spaces. If a player attempts alternative king movements, her opponent will surely cry foul. And if that player insists on continually breaking the rules, the game will quickly devolve into chaos and become unplayable.

Benjamin Franklin wrote an essay titled *On the Morals of Chess,* and he makes this point clear.

> *"If it is agreed to play according the strict rules, then those rules are to be exactly observed by both parties; and should not be insisted on for one side, while deviated from by the other; for this is not equitable."*(1)

When players who know and understand the rules of Chess sit down to play a game, they don't have to spend hours pointing out the limitations of every piece. To say a king can move one space in any direction logically excludes all other movement. The rules don't have to explicitly list every single illegal move. They don't have to explain that a king may not move two spaces. Three spaces. Four spaces. Et al.

The rules prohibit anything imaginable not explicitly allowed.

Now, imagine the following scenario in our Chess game. A player redefines "space" as it applies to the king, claiming the rule doesn't really mean adjacent space; therefore, a player can move his King to *any* space on the board with each move. I suppose we would call this the living, breathing Chess rulebook. It can adapt for the times and the needs of the game, right?

Ludicrous, isn't it? It would become impossible to play Chess if players were allowed to take such liberties. The integrity of the game depends on a uniform understanding and application of the rules.

The same logic holds true when considering a political system. People can only live together and cooperate in a society with an agreed upon, consistently applied set of rules. We call this the "rule of law." The principle roots itself in the idea that no individual or institution stands above the law, and that the rules apply equally to all people in any given situation. Rule of law creates a bulwark against arbitrary power, whether wielded by a totalitarian leader, advanced by mob rule, or exercised by duly elected legislators.

Aristotle wrote, "It is more proper that law should govern than any one of the citizens: upon the same principle, if it is advantageous to place the supreme power in some particular persons, they should be appointed to be only guardians, and the servants of the laws."(2)

The Constitution stands as the supreme law of the land in the United States – the authoritative rulebook. In order for the American system of government to work, we *must* adhere to the Constitution; we must uphold the rule of law. That means applying the Constitution every issue, every time, no exceptions, no excuses. Otherwise, we will find ourselves subject to the whims of those who hold political power. The Constitution was intended to restrain and limit power, thus protecting the lives, liberty and property of all citizens. The U.S system was set up in such a way as to place checks and balances on power. Every high school civics student learns about the intended separation of powers between the judicial, executive and legislative branches. These same students generally fail to learn that the framers also intended a division of power between the state governments and the general United States government. The framers intended the states to serve as a check on overreaching federal power. As we looked at in the introduction, James Madison summarized this division of power in Federalist 45, pointing out that powers delegated to the federal government were "few and defined." Those left to the several states, "numerous and indefinite."

As we've seen, the Constitution creates a general government and delegates specific authority to it. In the same way defining the movement of various pieces on a chess board logically excludes all other movements; the enumeration of certain powers in the Constitution logically excludes all powers not listed. *Designato unius est exclusio alterius* – a legal maxim meaning, "the designation of one is the exclusion of the other." In order for the Republic to operate in a fair and equitable matter, governmental powers must remain bound by the "rulebook." Congress can't simply take on additional powers, even if legislators think it may serve the public good. The president can't simply do whatever he pleases just because he's the president. The Constitution limits his role and power to a carefully prescribed sphere. When the federal government usurps its authority and exercises powers never granted, the Republic devolves into lawlessness.

Nineteenth century legal scholar St. George Tucker argued in his essay *Of the Several Forms of Government* that people lose basic liberty under a government built on usurpation of power.

> "But no people can ever be free, whose government is founded upon the usurpation of their sovereign rights; for by the act of usurpation, the sovereignty is transferred from the people, in whom alone it can legitimately reside, to those who by that act have manifested a determination to oppress them."(3)

Tucker's words seem eerily prophetic today.

> "If in a limited government, the public functionaries exceed the limits which the constitution prescribes to their powers, every such act is an act of usurpation in the government, and, as such, treason against the sovereignty of the people, which is thus endeavored to be subverted and transferred to the usurpers."(4)

And here we are today.

But how do we know what those enumerated powers really mean? How do we determine the extent of powers delegated?

The only rational way to understand the Constitution lies in an interpretive process known as originalism. To read the Constitution through an originalist framework simply means we seek to understand the ratifiers' original intent – what they believed they were agreeing to. Otherwise, meaning becomes a moving target, subject to the changes in language and societal assumptions over time.

In a letter to Richard Henry Lee dated June 1824, Madison affirms this view of constitutional interpretation.

> *"I entirely concur in the propriety of resorting to the sense in which the Constitution was accepted and ratified by the nation. In that sense alone it is the legitimate Constitution. And if that be not the guide in expounding it, there can be no security for a consistent and stable, more than for a faithful exercise of its powers. If the meaning of the text be sought in the changeable meaning of the words composing it, it is evident that the shape and attributes of the Government must partake of the changes to which the words and phrases of all living languages are constantly subject. What a metamorphosis would be produced in the code of law if all its ancient phraseology were to be taken in its modern sense!"(5)*

Judges use a similar process when settling contract disputes today. They attempt to ascertain what each party believed it was agreeing to at the time the contract was finalized. We're not talking about a simplistic literal reading of the words on the page. Understanding what the ratifiers intended takes some research and digging. On the other hand, a mystical veil of historical fog doesn't obscure their view of constitutional powers. We have records of the ratification debates and the ratifying instruments themselves. We also have the Federalist Papers and other documents written by supporters, used to "sell" the Constitution to ratifying convention delegates and the population at large. These essays were akin to the window sticker on a used car, explaining exactly what the ratifiers were "buying." We also have countless letters written by framers and ratifiers to guide our understanding. With a little work, you will find the original meaning of the Constitution easily determined and understandable. Thomas Jefferson himself advocated this process of constitutional interpretation.

> *"On every question of construction let us carry ourselves back to the time when the Constitution was adopted, recollect the spirit manifested in the debates, and instead of trying what meaning may be squeezed out of the text, or intended against it, conform to the probable one in which it was passed."*(6)

Ultimately, the ratifying conventions hold the key to the meaning of the Constitution. It was the ratifiers who agreed to establish the new government and gave the Constitution its authority, and their understanding reveals the extent of power that the people delegated to the new federal system. As the years went by, many proponents of a strong national government argued for expanded powers, pointing to the debates in the Philadelphia Convention. As the framers hammered out the Constitution, many argued for expansive central power. James Madison himself tried numerous times to give Congress a veto power over all state laws. Those hoping to expand the scope of federal power later argued that these debates revealed intent to give the general government more sweeping powers. Madison said, no, the ratifiers' understanding governs the meaning. Constitutional historian Kevin Gutzman paraphrases Madison's assertion.

> *"Some had committed the 'error' of 'ascribing to the intention of the Convention which formed the Constitution, an undue ascendancy in expounding it.' The authoritative source, he said, was not the Philadelphia Convention, but the 'State Conventions which gave it all the validity & authority it possesses.'* (7)

As we saw in the last chapter, the ratifying instruments clearly indicate the ratifying conventions believed they were creating a federal government with limited, enumerated powers, all other authority remaining with the states and the people.

One must also consider the nature of the people and the times that gave birth to the Constitution. In his book *The Original Constitution, What it Actually Said and Meant*, Robert Natelson points out the importance of keeping in mind the core values and philosophical world view shared by the founders. They were by no means homogeneous in their thinking, but the founders did generally agree on some basic tenants. These include the individual right to life, liberty and property; cognizance of the danger of concentrated government power; and a belief in decentralization and fiduciary government – meaning that government officials serve as trustee, bound by standards imposed on fiduciaries, including staying within imposed limits and working for the interests of the people. (8)

When considering these core values, it becomes clear that the founders intended to create a system that would protect the rights of the individual and limit the power of the government. We should always read the Constitution within that framework.

St. George Tucker explained how to view federal power in *View of the Constitution of the United States*, the first extended, systematic commentary on the Constitution after ratification. It was published in 1803 and served as an important handbook for American law students, lawyers, judges, jurists and statesmen for the first half of the 19th century.

> *"The powers delegated to the federal government, are, in all cases, to receive the most strict construction that the instrument will bear, where the rights of a state or of the people, either collectively or individually, may be drawn in question."(9)*

For the most part, modern "legal minds" have completely abandoned this fundamental principle of construction, instead reading the Constitution to grant the maximum amount of power to the federal government. As a result, the U.S. system has morphed into something inconceivable to the framers. Instead of a federal government exercising a few enumerated powers, the feds now enjoy nearly unlimited, undefined authority over every aspect of our lives. And the authority of the states, which Madison said would extend to "all objects concerning the lives, liberties and properties of the people, and the internal order, improvement and prosperity of the states," now extends to only a few narrowly defined spheres.

Progressives have taken the federal system created by the framers and completely flipped it on its head. They've managed to dramatically expand federal power through the misuse of a few key constitutional clauses: the supremacy clause, the necessary and proper clause, the general welfare clause, and the commerce clause.

Looking at the intended meaning of each of these key constitutional clauses will help properly define the proper powers of the federal government and will serve as an example of proper constitutional interpretation.

Supremacy Clause

We find the supremacy clause in Article VI.

> *"This Constitution, and the Laws of the United States which shall be made in Pursuance thereof; and all Treaties made, or which shall be made, under the Authority of the United States, shall be the supreme Law of the Land."*

Opponents of nullification, almost without fail, appeal to the Supremacy Clause to argue states lack the power to resist any federal act. In a June 23, 2011, op-ed criticizing a New Jersey nullification bill that would criminalize implementation of the Patient Protection and

Affordable Care Act, the Star-Ledger editorial board wrote, "On one level, the tactic of making it a crime to follow the law speaks of an Alice-in-Wonderland approach, where up is down and black is white. On another level, it reveals ignorance about the U.S. Constitution, which clearly defines the supremacy of federal law."

The argument appears sound on the surface. The Constitution does stipulate that federal law stands supreme. But does this give Congress carte blanche power to pass any old act it wants without any restrictions? Clearly not. To read the Supremacy Clause in that way ignores a key phrase – *in pursuance thereof*. In reality, only acts passed in pursuance of the Constitution stand as legitimate laws. An unconstitutional act, by definition, is illegal, null and void.

In the card game Spades, the ace of spades serves as the ultimate trump card. It beats every other card and automatically wins any trick when played. The ace of spades reigns supreme in the Spades game. But to call the ace supreme in a game of Uno is utter nonsense. An ace has no place in an Uno game. The ace's "authority" only exists within its proper sphere - the Spades game. In the same way, a federal act only carries authority within its proper sphere, defined by the enumerated powers delegated by the Constitution. Calling an unconstitutional act the supreme law of the land is just as absurd as playing an ace in a game of Uno.

Tucker addressed the supremacy clause in *View of the Constitution of the United States.*

"It may seem extraordinary, that a people jealous of their liberty, and not insensible of the allurement of power, should have entrusted the federal government with such extensive authority as this article conveys: controlling not only the acts of their ordinary legislatures, but their very constitutions, also.

"The most satisfactory answer seems to be, that the powers entrusted to the federal government being all positive, enumerated, defined, and limited to particular objects; and those objects such as relate more immediately to the intercourse with foreign nations, or the

relation in respect to war or peace, in which we may stand with them; there can, in these respects, be little room for collision, or interference between "the states, whose jurisdiction may be regarded as confided to their own domestic concerns, and the United States, who have no right to interfere, or exercise a power in any case not delegated to them, or absolutely necessary to the execution of some delegated power.

"That, as this control cannot possibly extend beyond those objects to which the federal government is competent, under the constitution, and under the declaration contained in the twelfth article (Tenth Amendment), so neither ought the laws, or even the constitution of any state to impede the operation of the federal government in any case within the limits of its constitutional powers. That a law limited to such objects as may be authorized by the constitution, would, under the true construction of this clause, be the supreme law of the land; **but a law not limited to those objects, or not made pursuant to the constitution, would not be the supreme law of the land, but an act of usurpation, and consequently void.**" (Emphasis added)(10)

Necessary and Proper Clause

The final power granted to Congress in Article 1, Sec. 8 is:

> "To make all Laws which shall be necessary and
> proper for carrying into Execution the foregoing
> Powers, and all other Powers vested by this
> Constitution in the Government of the United States,
> or in any Department or Officer thereof."

We know this as the necessary and proper clause. Some commonly call it the "elastic clause." Again, progressive legal theorists use this power to justify all kinds of expansive federal action never contemplated by the framers.

Legal documents delegating power commonly contain a necessary and proper clause. And it has a precise, specific definition. Basically, it allows an agent to exercise powers not explicitly spelled out in the legal document, but necessary to exercise the specific authority given to him.

For example, let's say I write out a contract granting you the authority to run my grocery store. I don't need to specify that you have the power to pay a guy to clean the floors, or hire a mechanic to fix a freezer when it goes down. Those powers are necessary and proper to running a grocery store. But necessary and proper powers don't give you the right to give away all of the food items in my store and turn it into a pornography shop.

As the framers understood the concept, any necessary and proper power remains constrained by specific criteria. The power must be:

1. Necessary to carry out the original purpose – like purchasing corn from a farmer to sell in the grocery store.
2. A customary way of carrying out the original purpose. The guy running my grocery couldn't get rid of all the food and sell porno because that would clearly not constitute a customary way of running a grocery store
3. An incidental power can never rise to a level greater than the original power delegated. My grocery store manager would have the authority to pay a mechanic for fixing the broken freezer. But he wouldn't have the power to sell the building and invest the money in the stock market for me. (11)

Necessary and proper powers do not add anything to the authority already delegated to Congress. They do not create any new powers. The clause simply reaffirms that the federal government possesses the flexibility to exercise the enumerated power already delegated.

Nothing more.

Nothing less.

In Federalist 33, Alexander Hamilton defended the supremacy, and necessary and proper clause against Anti-Federalists who argued that they could be construed to grant additional, expansive powers to the general government.

> *"It may be affirmed with perfect confidence that the constitutional operation of the intended government would be precisely the same, if these clauses were*

entirely obliterated, as if they were repeated in every article. They are only declaratory of a truth which would have resulted by necessary and unavoidable implication from the very act of constituting a federal government, and vesting it with certain specified powers."

Some argue for a broader reading of necessary and proper, asserting that in the name of efficiency, the federal government may exercise additional power if it makes achieving a constitutional end more convenient. Thomas Jefferson addressed this expansive reading of necessary and proper.

"The Constitution allows only the means which are 'necessary,' not those which are merely 'convenient' for effecting the enumerated powers. If such a latitude of construction be allowed to this phrase as to give any non-enumerated power, it will go to everyone, for there is not one which ingenuity may not torture into a convenience in some instance or other, to some one of so long a list of enumerated powers. It would swallow up all the delegated powers, and reduce the whole to one power, as before observed. Therefore it was that the Constitution restrained them to the necessary means, that is to say, to those means without which the grant of power would be nugatory."(12)

Note Tucker's rule of construction implicit in Jefferson's explanation. We must always look at the powers delegated in the "most strict construction" possible, keeping in mind that the Constitution created a federal government exercising limited authority.

Finally, Virginia ratification convention delegate George Nicholas testified to the fact that the necessary and proper clause does nothing to expand powers during the ratification debates, attempting to soothe the minds of those who feared the federal government would take it that way.

*"Suppose it had been inserted at the end of every power, that they should have the power to make laws to carry that power into execution; would this have increased their powers? If therefore it could not have increased their powers, if placed at the end of each power, it cannot increase them at the end of all. This clause only enables them to carry into execution the powers given them, **but gives them no additional power.**"* (Emphasis added)(13)

General Welfare Clause

The General Welfare clause provides a third avenue for progressives wishing to expand federal power far beyond the intent of the framers. We find the clause in the opening line of Article I Sec. 8.

"The Congress shall have Power To lay and collect Taxes, Duties, Imposts and Excises, to pay the Debts and provide for the common Defence and general Welfare of the United States;"

The phrase "general welfare" also appears in the Constitution's preamble.

"We the People of the United States, in Order to form a more perfect Union, establish Justice, insure domestic Tranquility, provide for the common defence, promote the general Welfare, and secure the Blessings of Liberty to ourselves and our Posterity, do ordain and establish this Constitution for the United States of America."

Progressives read this to mean that the federal government enjoys the power to do anything at all they define as promoting general welfare. This clause typically serves as the justification for programs like Social Security, Medicare, nationalized health care, FEMA, and federal meddling in education.

Huffington Post columnist Paul Abrams demonstrated this line of thinking in a March 9, 2011, piece.

> *"Article 1, Section 8, Clause 1 grants the United States government the unqualified and unlimited power to raise and spend money, for example, to: provide healthcare for the elderly (or for everyone); provide old-age pension; build roads, bridges, train tracks, airports, electric grids, libraries, swimming pools, housing; educate our children, re-train the unemployed, provide pre-school and day care; fund public health projects; invest in and conduct basic research; provide subsidies for agriculture; save the auto industry; create internets (sic); and, yes, Tea Party Senator Mike Lee (R-UT), even provide emergency aid from natural disasters, and so forth. All subsumed under the authority to spend for the general welfare."*

Abrams' assertion raises an important question. If the very first clause of Article 1 Sec. 8 grants unlimited and unqualified authority for the federal government to do any damn thing it wants, why did the framers bother to waste ink enumerating all of those other powers? I mean, they were handwriting the thing for goodness sake. Seems to me an economy of words would have definitely been in order.

James Madison made this very point, albeit much more eloquently.

> *"With respect to the two words 'general welfare,' I have always regarded them as qualified by the detail of powers connected with them. To take them in a literal and unlimited sense would be a metamorphosis of the Constitution into a character which there is a host of proofs was not contemplated by its creators."(14)*

You can look to the ratifying conventions for those proofs. In fact, the anti-federalists feared that people like Abrams would come along and make the very argument he advances. The federalists assured them this wouldn't happen – that the general government's powers were in fact limited and defined. The states ratified the Constitution based on these assurances. Even Alexander Hamilton, the framer most in favor of expansive federal power, conceded as much in Federalist 83.

> *"This specification of particulars [the 18 enumerated powers of Article I, Section 8] evidently excludes all pretension to a general legislative authority, because an affirmative grant of special powers would be absurd as well as useless if a general authority was intended."*

Madison specifically addressed the Anti-Federalist fears in Federalist 41. Keep in mind this was how supporters "sold" the Constitution to the public.

> *"It has been urged and echoed, that the power "to lay and collect taxes, duties, imposts, and excises, to pay the debts, and provide for the common defense and general welfare of the United States," amounts to an unlimited commission to exercise every power which may be alleged to be necessary for the common defense or general welfare. No stronger proof could be given of the distress under which these writers labor for objections, than their stooping to such a misconstruction. Had no other enumeration or definition of the powers of the Congress been found in the Constitution, than the general expressions just cited, the authors of the objection might have had some color for it; though it would have been difficult to find a reason for so awkward a form of describing an authority to legislate in all possible case."*

He goes on to write:

> ***"For what purpose could the enumeration of particular powers be inserted, if these and all others were meant to be included in the preceding general power?*** *Nothing is more natural nor common than*

first to use a general phrase, and then to explain and qualify it by a recital of particulars. But the idea of an enumeration of particulars which neither explain nor qualify the general meaning, and can have no other effect than to confound and mislead, is an absurdity, which, as we are reduced to the dilemma of charging either on the authors of the objection or on the authors of the Constitution, we must take the liberty of supposing, had not its origin with the latter." (Emphasis added)

Madison further illuminated the intended meaning of the general welfare clause in a letter to Edmund Pendleton dated 1793, pointing out that the phrase was lifted from the Articles of Confederation and was intended to retain its meaning in the new Constitution.

"If Congress can do whatever in their discretion can be done by money, and will promote the general welfare, the Government is no longer a limited one possessing enumerated powers, but an indefinite one subject to particular exceptions. It is to be remarked that the phrase out of which this doctrine is elaborated, is copied from the old articles of Confederation, where it was always understood as nothing more than a general caption to the specified powers, and it is a fact that it was preferred in the new instrument for that very reason as less liable than any other to misconstruction."

So, the words general welfare must mean something other than a grant of power for Congress to do whatever it pleased. What exactly did the framers mean?

Two words in the clause hold the key. **General** and **common.** The phrase simply means that any tax collected must be collected to the benefit of the United States as a whole, not for partial or sectional (i.e. special) interests. In fact, the Tenth Amendment makes clear that the power to pursue the things Abrams advocates, like health care for the elderly, power grids and internets (sic) - all objects which, in the ordinary course of affairs, concern the lives, liberties and properties of the people, and the internal order, improvement and prosperity of the State - remains with the states respectively or the people.

Power creep through *the general* welfare clause began long ago. During a debate on federal funding for a relief effort benefiting St. Domingo Refugees, the Congressional record of Jan. 10, 1794 records Madison's objections.

> *"Mr. MADISON remarked, that the government of the United States is a definite government, confined to specified objects. It is not like the state governments, whose powers are more general. Charity is no part of the legislative duty of the government. It would puzzle any gentleman to lay his finger on any part of the Constitution which would authorize the government to interpose in the relief of the St. Domingo sufferers."*

Commerce Clause

The final weapon in the progressive arsenal used to expand federal power is the Commerce Clause

"To regulate Commerce with foreign Nations, and among the several States, and with the Indian Tribes."

The Commerce Clause was originally intended to give the federal government power to maintain free and open trade between the states, and between the United States and other nations. It was basically meant to give the federal government the power to prevent states from restricting trade through levying tariffs on neighbors. In other words, the feds have the authority to keep Tennessee from slapping a fee on bourbon imported from Kentucky. It was a power intended to protect free and robust trade. The commerce clause also gave the federal government the authority to pursue a unified trade policy with other nations, as opposed to each state enforcing its own policy. Some define it as a power to "make trade regular." James Madison explained the intent of the Commerce Clause.

> "It is very certain that [the commerce clause] grew
> out of the abuse of the power by the importing States
> in taxing the non-importing, and was intended as a
> negative and preventive provision against injustice
> among the States themselves, rather than as a power
> to be used for the positive purposes of the General
> Government."

But progressives did exactly that – turned the power into something to be used for the positive purposes of the general government. The Supreme Court ruling in *Wickard v. Filburn* back in 1942 flipped the Commerce Clause on its head. The SCOTUS ruled that the federal government could regulate a farmer growing wheat on his own land for his own consumption, wheat that never left the farm, much less the state, because the farmer's activity could have a "substantial effect on interstate commerce."

> "Whether the subject of the regulation in question
> was 'production,' 'consumption,' or 'marketing' is,
> therefore, not material for purposes of deciding the
> question of federal power before us. That an activity
> is of local character may help in a doubtful case to
> determine whether Congress intended to reach it....
> **But even if appellee's activity be local and though it
> may not be regarded as commerce, it may still,
> whatever its nature, be reached by Congress if it
> exerts a substantial economic effect on interstate
> commerce** and this irrespective of whether such effect
> is what might at some earlier time have been defined
> as 'direct' or 'indirect.'" (Emphasis added)

Further, modern scholars have morphed and broadened the meaning of "commerce" into something alien to the framers' understanding of the word. Commerce basically meant trade – the act of exchanging goods. Commerce power also extended to regulation of the transportation system, shipping, and interstate and international waterways. But the Commerce Clause was never intended to give the federal government the power to regulate manufacturing, agriculture, labor laws, health care or a host of other activities claimed by progressives. Constitutional scholar and author of *The Original Constitution: What it Actually Meant and Said*, Robert Natelson examined the legal constitutional meaning of commerce. He scoured 17th and 18th century case law, legal works and legal dictionaries, as well as lay usage of the word. His research showed commerce was almost exclusively used in connection with trade – not the broader range of economic activities the Supreme Court uses in *Wickard*. In a scholarly paper titled *The Legal Meaning of "Commerce" in the Commerce Clause*, Natelson writes:

> "Commerce benefited agriculture and manufacture by circulating their products, but it did not include agriculture or manufacture. Jurists compared commerce to an enormous circulatory system, carrying articles throughout the entire Body Politic, as the blood in the human body carries oxygen and nourishment. Thus, like the American Founders, English lawyers and judges understood the tight interrelationship between commerce and other parts of the economy, yet they were careful to distinguish them conceptually."(16)

According to Georgetown University Law professor Randy E. Barnett, Madison's notes from the Philadelphia Convention bear this out.

> "In Madison's notes for the Constitutional Convention, the term 'commerce' appears thirty-four times in the speeches of the delegates. Eight of these are unambiguous references to commerce with foreign nations which can only consist of trade. In every other instance, the terms 'trade' or 'exchange' could be substituted for the term 'commerce' with the apparent meaning of the statement preserved. In no instance is the term 'commerce' clearly used to refer to 'any gainful activity' or anything broader than trade. One congressional power proposed by

Madison, but not ultimately adopted, suggests that the delegates shared the limited meaning of 'commerce' described in Johnson's dictionary. Madison proposed to grant Congress the power 'to establish public institutions, rewards, and immunities for the promotion of agriculture, commerce, trades and manufactures,' strongly suggesting that the members understood the term 'commerce' to mean trade or exchange, distinct from the productive processes that made the things to be traded."(17)

Barnett goes on to point out that the records of the ratifying conventions reveal the same narrow definition of commerce.

"In the records of the Massachusetts convention, the word 'commerce' is used nineteen times--every use consistent with it meaning trade, mostly foreign trade; and no use clearly indicating a broader meaning. The most explicit distinction was made by Thomas Dawes, a prominent revolutionary and legislator, who began his discussion on the importance of the national taxation powers. 'We have suffered,' said he, 'for want of such authority in the federal head. This will be evident if we take a short view of our agriculture, commerce, and manufactures.' He then expounded at some length, giving separate attention to each of these activities and the beneficial effect the Constitution would have on them. Under the heading of 'commerce,' he referred to 'our own domestic traffic that passes from state to state.'"(18)

Some modern jurists acknowledge that the framers and ratifiers define commerce in the limited sense of trade, but argue the increased sophistication of America's economic system necessitates deeper federal involvement, and they justify the expansion of power on the necessary and proper clause. Natelson takes this idea on in a piece published on the Tenth Amendment Center website.

"The second argument for an almost unlimited Commerce Power currently prevails on the U.S. Supreme Court. (Don't let anyone tell you the present court is "conservative" on such matters.) This argument acknowledges that when the Founders wrote "Commerce," they meant only trade and a few allied activities, such as navigation.

"But it goes on to say that modern economic life, unlike life during the Founding Era, is highly interdependent, so it is now "necessary and proper" for Congress to regulate everything that substantially affects commerce.

"But this argument also ignores history. Economic interdependence is nothing new: the promoters of the Constitution themselves emphasized it. But they also assured the public that, interdependent or not, most activities could be regulated only by the states."(19)

Once again, we see progressive legal theory and court precedent ripping the meaning from the Constitution, fundamentally transforming the federal government from one of limited, defined powers to one of limitless, undefined authority over virtually every aspect of life.

Conclusion

When we take the time to read and study, understanding what the Constitution means really poses few problems. We don't need law degrees or years of formal classroom instruction. We just need to always remember the underlying premise – the Constitution delegates specific powers, and anything not given remains with the states or the people. We must always read it assuming the strictest limitation on federal power. That was the clear intent of the ratifiers. Always keep the words of Madison in Federalist 45 in mind when considering the extent of federal power. "The powers delegated to the federal government by the proposed constitution are few and defined. Those which remain in the State governments are numerous and indefinite." The colonists fought a long, bloody war against great odds to free themselves from centralized power. Why would they then proceed to set up a government with far reaching powers? Those who insist the federal government should wield wide-ranging authority lose the intellectual argument from square one.

When one accepts the limits placed on federal power, it logically follows that some mechanism must exist to stop overreach. The states and the people must possess a way to halt the feds when they try to exercise powers not delegated. Otherwise, the Constitution is simply a cool looking piece of parchment resting inside a glass case.

That's where nullification comes in. The states, as parties to the Constitution, can simply say, "No!" to unconstitutional federal acts. Their power is implicit in the constitutional system created by the framers.

But a question remains unresolved. Who decides what is or isn't constitutional?

5

SO, WHO DECIDES?

Once we agree that the Constitution means what it means, a problem remains.

Who decides?

Who decides how the Constitution applies to a specific act? Who decides whether a given regulation passed by Congress fits within its enumerated powers? Who decides if a president possesses the constitutional authority to issue and enforce an executive order?

Most Americans will quickly answer, "Why the Supreme Court does, of course."

But who ensures that the Supreme Court remains within its constitutionally delegated powers? And what prevents a runaway court from declaring any number of things, clearly incompatible with the Constitution, perfectly legal and valid? Do we really believe that nine politically connected and appointed judges wear a mantle of infallibility?

Littleton Waller Tazwell served in the U.S. House and Senate, and as the 26th governor of Virginia. He wrote a systematic response to Andrew Jackson's 1832 Proclamation Regarding Nullification. Jackson declared nullification unconstitutional and argued that the judicial branch was the proper arbiter in cases involving questions of constitutionality. Tazwell disagreed because he understood the imperfect nature of judges and the danger of granting the judiciary such sweeping power.

> "For the Judiciary of the United States, I entertain at least as much respect as I do for any other Judiciary. I will not say more; and I cannot say less. With the individual Judges, I have nothing to do. They shall all be, if any one thinks so, what some of them certainly are, "like Mansfield wise, and as old Foster just." But all must know that the robes of office do not cover angels, but mere men, as prone to err, as any other men of equal intelligence, of equal purity, and of equal constancy. We all know, too, that some of the supreme Judges of the United States have not thought it unbecoming their high places, to accept Foreign Missions, to present themselves as candidates for other offices, and to enter into newspaper disquisitions upon party topics. I do not mean to blame them for such things, but merely to shew from such facts, that the rights of sovereign States, when assailed by the government of the United States, could not be safely confided to a forum so constituted, even if it was possible that it could take cognizance of the subject."(1)

A quick reading of the decision in *Dred Scott v. Sanford* (1857) should cause any reasonable person to question the assumption of judicial infallibility, and the wisdom of granting judges the definitive and final say in all cases. In essence, the Supreme Court declared black people inferior and that even free blacks were not citizens under the Constitution. In the majority opinion, Chief Justice Roger Taney argued that the framers of the Constitution held blacks were, "beings of an inferior order, and altogether unfit to associate with the white race, either in social or political relations, and so far inferior that they had no rights which the white man was bound to respect."

The court reasoned that since black people - even those not held in slavery - were not citizens and possessed no rights, Scott had no standing to sue in court.

> "The question before us is, whether the class of persons described in the plea in abatement [people of Aftican (sic) ancestry] compose a portion of this people, and are constituent members of this sovereignty? We think they are not, and that they are not included, and were not intended to be included, under the word 'citizens' in the Constitution, and can therefore claim none of the rights and privileges which that instrument provides for and secures to citizens of the United States. On the contrary, they were at that time considered as a subordinate and inferior class of beings, who had been subjugated by the dominant race, and, whether emancipated or not, yet remained subject to their authority, and had no rights or privileges but such as those who held the power and the Government might choose to grant them."

The Court could have ended the decision there, but it took the next step and lectured the nation, going on to assert that granting Scott's petition for freedom would unleash all kinds of evil upon the United States.

> *"It would give to persons of the negro race, who were recognized as citizens in any one State of the Union, the right to enter every other State whenever they pleased, singly or in companies, without pass or passport, and without obstruction, to sojourn there as long as they pleased, to go where they pleased at every hour of the day or night without molestation, unless they committed some violation of law for which a white man would be punished; and it would give them the full liberty of speech in public and in private upon all subjects upon which its own citizens might speak; to hold public meetings upon political affairs, and to keep and carry arms wherever they went. And all of this would be done in the face of the subject race of the same color, both free and slaves, and inevitably producing discontent and insubordination among them, and endangering the peace and safety of the State."*

This august body that most Americans depend on to dispense justice, protect minority rights and serve as the final authority on all things constitutional resorted to brazen, unadulterated fear-mongering.

Infallible, authoritative and always reliable to serve justice, eh?

So, if we can't count on the Court to consistently rule without error or prejudice, why should it serve as the final arbiter on the extent of federal power?

For the last 100 years, most Americans have assumed the federal court system, and ultimately the Supreme Court, stands as the final arbiter in any constitutional controversy. But who made the federal courts King?

The Constitution certainly didn't. Take a moment and go look for the clause in the Constitution that delegates to the Supreme Court the power to serve as the sole and final authority on what is or isn't constitutional. You won't find it, because it does not exist. The Constitution tasks the Court with "judging cases."

So, who placed the Supreme Court at the pinnacle of Constitutional interpretation?

Why, the Supreme Court itself did!

In 1958, the SCOTUS declared "constitutional law," as determined by the federal court system, the supreme law of the land, on equal footing with the Constitution itself. The Supreme Court set itself on its own throne in its ruling in *Cooper v. Aaron*, a case relating to school desegregation.

> "Article VI of the Constitution makes the Constitution
> the 'supreme Law of the Land.' In 1803, Chief Justice
> Marshall, speaking for a unanimous Court, referring
> to the Constitution as 'the fundamental and
> paramount law of the nation,' declared in the notable
> case of Marbury v. Madison, 1 Cranch 137, 177, 2
> L.Ed. 60, that 'It is emphatically the province and duty
> of the judicial department to say what the law is.' This
> decision declared the basic principle that the federal
> judiciary is supreme in the exposition of the law of the
> Constitution, and that principle has ever since been
> respected by this Court and the Country as a
> permanent and indispensable feature of our
> constitutional system."

The Cooper decision hangs on *Marbury v. Madison* (1803). The Marshall Court ruled the *Judiciary Act of 1789* unconstitutional, thus establishing the Court's power of judicial review. This was the first time the Supreme Court used the power of judicial review. And in a sense, the court did bestow upon itself the power by its exercise thereof. But in fact, the idea that courts could invalidate unconstitutional law pre-dated the Marbury ruling and even the

Enten=

ratification of the Constitution. Alexander Hamilton discussed the concept in Federalist 78.

> "[T]he courts were designed to be an intermediate body between the people and the legislature, in order, among other things, to keep the latter within the limits assigned to their authority. The interpretation of the laws is the proper and peculiar province of the courts. A constitution is, in fact, and must be regarded by the judges as, a fundamental law. It, therefore, belongs to them to ascertain its meaning, as well as the meaning of any particular act proceeding from the legislative body. If there should happen to be an irreconcilable variance between the two, that which has the superior obligation and validity ought, of course, to be preferred; or, in other words, the Constitution ought to be preferred to the statute, the intention of the people to the intention of their agents."

So, nobody understanding the nature of the judicial system should question that the court possesses the power to declare an act unconstitutional, and the judiciary rightly has the final say in a dispute between the various branches of the federal government. Its rulings stand supreme only in those *cases* the Constitution gives it the power to judge. The Court checks legislative and executive power. But the question remains: does the Court possess **sole** authority to declare an act unconstitutional when a dispute arises between the federal government, and the states or the people?

Or more simply put: does a single branch of the federal government serve as the sole judge of the extent of the federal government's own power? Does the created get to dictate to the creator the condition of its own existence?

To answer, "Yes," opens the door to tyranny, because such a system leaves no option for the states or the people to exercise in their defense should all three branches conspire to impose an unconstitutional measure. In essence, those who advocate supreme judicial authority tell the states and the people to "sit down and shut up" if a federal court puts its stamp of approval on an unconstitutional act. The notion invalidates the Constitution as the supreme law of the land, instead vesting that power in the pronouncement of five out of nine judges. And that seems absurd in light of the framers' deep distrust of concentrated power.

Judge Able P. Upshur, a Virginia politician and jurist who also served as U.S. Secretary of State and War, explained the intended relationship between the Supreme Court and the States in his 1833 publication *Commentaries on the Constitution of the United States.*

> "The Federal Government is the creature of the States. It is not a party to the Constitution, but the result of it – the creation of that agreement which was made by the States as parties. It is a mere agent, entrusted with limited powers for certain objects; which powers and objects are enumerated in the Constitution. Shall the agent be permitted to judge of the extent of his own powers, without reference to his constituent?"

The answer to Upshur's question is self-evident. To say, "Yes," is nonsensical.

The Constitution grants no enumerated power to the federal government for establishing a nationalized health care system. Health care falls within the vast body of power left to the states respectively, or to the people, under the Tenth Amendment. But Congress insisted that the authority to implement the Patient Protection and Affordable Care Act flows from the Commerce and General Welfare clauses. As we have seen, the intended meaning of those two clauses does not grant any such authority. Even the Supreme Court recognized that reality in its 2012 ruling. But the court still managed to find a way around it. They magically turned a penalty into a tax.

Justice John Roberts first argued that requiring an American to purchase health insurance stretches an already elastic commerce clause past the breaking point. Can't do that. He then argued that the "necessary and proper clause" provides no wiggle room allowing the feds to force Americans to buy health insurance. Can't do that. But behold, Roberts found one last refuge to safely place this oh-so-important federal power: the taxing authority.

With some verbal doublespeak that would make George Orwell proud, Roberts turned a penalty into a tax and then declared the whole thing a perfectly valid exercise of federal power. In essence, the federal government can't force you to buy health insurance, but it can twist your arm to "encourage" you to buy health insurance. The Court completely ignored the fact that the authority to tax does not include the authority to spend. The enumerated powers of Congress do not include spending money to manage a national health care program.

Does the SCOTUS ruling really mean the federal government wields the power to create a health care system for every state and individual in America, and the authority to force every citizen to take part? Does the ruling negate the actual meaning of the Constitution? Just because five of nine judges say so, do we accept that the federal government possesses this sweeping power – the authority to dictate that every American must participate in a given economic activity on the federal government's terms?

And again, do we *really* believe that one branch of the federal government should get the final say in a dispute involving the federal government?

Seems like a fox guarding the henhouse kind of scenario, doesn't it?

In a hockey game, both teams defer to the referees. They serve as the final authorities on the interpretation and enforcement of the rules. But what happens in a refless game?

Growing up, kids in my neighborhood often got together and played sandlot games. Football, soccer, kickball. You name it; we played it. We made a few phone calls, met up at a vacant lot, chose sides and locked horns in epic matchups until our moms started calling us home. And I don't ever remember having a referee. It fell upon the shoulders of the players on each team to interpret and enforce the rules.

No doubt, we often debated a close call.

"He's out!"

"No, he's not! He made it by a mile!"

"Did not, cheater. He was wayyyy out!"

And on it went. But somehow, we managed to work things out. Generally, somebody eventually relented and play continued. Or a kid with a bit cooler head from one team or the other stepped up and admitted the obvious.

"Yeah, honestly, he was out."

Every once in a while, only a "do-over" sufficed. We resolved it different ways at different times, but we always managed to play out the game.

Now, imagine for a moment that during one of our pick-up games, we picked a member of one team or the other to serve as the ref - the final authority on all calls and disputes. Do you think for one second that the guys on the dark shirt team would accept one of the light jersey players as the all-time ref? I mean, most of us were pretty good kids. Honest and forthright. Most of the time. He would call the game fairly without an ounce of bias.

Right?

Or do you think the players on the Washington Redskins would accept a Dallas Cowboys player as the referee in one of their bi-annual divisional rivalry games?

Of course not!

Nobody with an ounce of sense would accept that scenario. Yet millions of Americans, including legal experts, political pundits and learned professors, think the U.S. system should operate exactly that way. One branch of the federal government gets the final say in a dispute between the federal government, and the states and the people.

How's that working out for us?

About the same as you might expect if a member of the opposing team served as ref in your driveway basketball game.

The Court almost never rules in a way that limits federal power. In fact, between the founding and 2002, the Court ruled only 158 federal acts unconstitutional in whole or in part, according to the Government Printing Office. Considering the amount of legislation passed by Congress through the history of the Republic- not too impressive! Do you really believe every act Congress passed in that 213 year span fell within its constitutionally enumerated powers? Do you honestly believe every presidential executive order, every bureaucratic regulation and every action taken by every federal agency rested perfectly within the powers granted the Constitution?

Me neither.

The Court looks out for its own.

Think about it: we expect the Supreme Court (part of the federal government), made up of nine justices, paid by the federal government, appointed by the president (part of the federal government) and approved by the Senate (part of the federal government) to overrule Congress (part of the federal government), or the president (part of the federal government), and thus limit the powers of the federal government.

Yeah. OK.

In fact, the courts almost always accept the federal government's ever expanding definition of its own power.

That fact makes some other check on federal power necessary. The federal government will not protect the people against itself. James Madison and Thomas Jefferson understood this. And they recognized this inherent conflict of interest. They refused to accept the notion that the Supreme Court stood as the final arbiter. In the Kentucky Resolutions of 1798, Jefferson wrote:

> "The government created by this compact (the Constitution) was not made the exclusive or final judge of the extent of the powers delegated to itself; since that would have made its discretion, and not the Constitution, the measure of its powers; but that, as in all other cases of compact among powers having no common judge, each party has an equal right to judge for itself, as well of infractions as of the mode and measure of redress."

Each party possesses an equal right to judge for itself, just like two opposing teams in those refless childhood games. Each team holds equal power and authority to interpret a rule and make a judgment. They must work it out together, as equals. Otherwise, one team clearly enjoys an unfair and unacceptable advantage.

James Madison makes this very point in Federalist No. 10.

"No man is allowed to be a judge in his own case, because his interest would certainly bias his judgment, and not improbably, corrupt his integrity."

Madison expanded on this idea in his Report of 1800, a defense of the Virginia Resolutions of 1798.

> "But it is objected that the judicial authority is to be regarded as the sole expositor of the Constitution, in the last resort; and it may be asked for what reason,

the declaration by the General Assembly, supposing it to be theoretically true, could be required at the present day and in so solemn a manner.

"On this objection it might be observed, first, that there may be instances of usurped power, which the forms of the Constitution would never draw within the control of the judicial department; secondly, that if the decision of the judiciary be raised above the authority of the sovereign parties to the Constitution, the decisions of the other departments, not carried by the forms of the Constitution before the judiciary, must be equally authoritative and final with the decisions of that department. But the proper answer to the objection is, that the resolution of the General Assembly relates to those great and extraordinary cases, in which all the forms of the Constitution may prove ineffectual against infractions dangerous to the essential rights of the parties to it. The resolution supposes that dangerous powers, not delegated, may not only be usurped and executed by the other departments, but that the judicial department also may exercise or sanction dangerous powers beyond the grant of the Constitution; and, consequently, that the ultimate right of the parties to the Constitution, to judge whether the compact has been dangerously violated, must extend to violations by one delegated authority, as well as by another; by the judiciary, as well as by the executive, or the legislature.

"However true, therefore, it may be, that the judicial department, is, in all questions submitted to it by the forms of the Constitution, to decide in the last resort, this resort must necessarily be deemed the last in relation to the authorities of the other departments of the government; not in relation to the rights of the parties to the constitutional compact, from which the judicial as well as the other departments hold their delegated trusts. On any other hypothesis, the delegation of judicial power would annul the

*authority delegating it; and the concurrence of this
department with the others in usurped powers, might
subvert for ever, and beyond the possible reach of any
rightful remedy, the very Constitution which all were
instituted to preserve."*

Jefferson and Madison based their argument on the concept of
power delegation, as we discussed in chapter three. The people
created the federal government through the states, and the people of
the states retained their sovereignty in all realms, except where
authority was delegated to the new general government. The states
stand as equal parties to a compact – or contract in more modern
language. To give the federal government absolute authority to
decide the extent of its own power would place the created above
the creator.

It doesn't make logical sense.

It would be like giving the bank absolute power to determine the
meaning of your mortgage terms. In a dispute, you would insist on a
neutral judge. But as Jefferson points out in the Kentucky Resolutions
of 1798, no common judge exists between the federal government
and the states. That leaves the power to decide in the hands of the
parties to the compact. To assume the framers intended the federal
government to stand as the final authority would essentially cede all
power to the federal government and destroy any notion of state
sovereignty, something the framers clearly never intended. Recall the
Virginia ratifying instrument. It declared the Commonwealth retained
the right to take back the powers delegated, "whensoever the same
shall be perverted to their injury or oppression and that every power
not granted thereby remains with them and at their will." Implicit in
that right is the power to determine when exactly the federal
government oversteps its authority to the injury or oppression of the
people of the state.

This idea is the cornerstone of nullification. The states serve as a
check on federal power.

St. George Tucker makes this case in *View of the Constitution of the United States*. Keep in mind this was the first book on United States constitutional law.

> "In the United States, the great and essential rights of the people are secured against legislative as well as executive ambition. ... They are secured, not by laws, only, which the legislature who makes them may repeal, and annul at its pleasure; but by constitutions, paramount to all laws: defining and limiting the powers of the legislature itself, and opposing barriers against encroachments, which it can not pass, without warning the people of their danger. Secondly, by that division, and distribution of power between the federal, and the state governments, by which each is in some degree made a check upon the excesses of the other. For although the states possess no constitutional negative upon the proceedings of the congress of the United States, yet it seems to be a just inference and conclusion, that as the powers of the federal government result from the compact to which the states are parties; and are limited by the plain sense of the instrument constituting that compact; they are no further valid, than as they are authorized by the grants enumerated therein: and, that in case of a deliberate, palpable, and dangerous exercise of other powers, not granted by that compact, the states, who are parties thereto, have the right, and are in duty bound, to interpose, for arresting the progress of the evil, and for maintaining within their respective limits, the authorities, rights, and liberties appertaining to them."(2)

To argue that federal courts stand as the final arbiter puts the federal government in the position of serving as a check upon itself, a nonsensical position.

Let's say you and I become embroiled in some kind of dispute, and I assert that my wife will make the final decision. Would you accept that? I mean, my wife is a wonderful woman. Very upstanding and fair-minded. In fact, she might decide things your way.

Every once in a while.

Maybe.

No. You would insist on a neutral judge. Or we would have to work out our differences together as equals. You certainly wouldn't accept my mom as judge. Not if you cared about winning your case. (3)

Opponents of nullification will argue that letting states judge for themselves will create unmanageable chaos, bedlam and anarchy. But will it? Really? And will it necessarily lead to insurmountable gridlock? If those childhood sandlot games provide any indication, I would have to answer, no. We always managed to work it out – together - as equal parties to the game. Sometime our team would give in and at other times the opposition would give. Looking back, the negotiations, (OK, the arguments) however heated they became, led to the correct call the vast majority of the time. Why? Because deep down we all knew the truth. We knew the kid was out, or safe, or out of bounds or whatever. And after all the yelling and blustering wound down, and we wearied ourselves arguing out of our own self-interest, the truth came out and we moved on to finish the game. In those rare occasions we honestly didn't know, or it was legitimately too close to call, we compromised with the good-old do-over.

That kind of give and take makes much more sense in a democratic republic than anointing a nine-judge panel the sole authority and granting them nearly unlimited power over the people. I mean, don't we, as Americans, value robust debate and democratic principles? Don't we scorn the idea of monarchy and oligarchy? It may prove messy at times, but government of, by and for the people sometimes gets messy. That's OK. And it's what our founders intended.

James Madison laid out the plan for dealing with federal overreach in Federalist 46. We looked at this in the introduction, but it demonstrates the intentionally contentious and messy nature of our system, and it deserves a second reading here.

"Should an unwarrantable measure of the federal government be unpopular in particular States, which would seldom fail to be the case, or even a warrantable measure be so, which may sometimes be the case, the means of opposition to it are powerful and at hand. The disquietude of the people; their repugnance and, perhaps refusal to cooperate with officers of the Union, the frowns of the executive magistracy of the State; the embarrassment created by legislative devices, which would often be added on such occasions, would oppose, in any State, very serious impediments; and were the sentiments of several adjoining States happen to be in Union, would present obstructions which the federal government would hardly be willing to encounter."

This scenario played out vividly during the nullification crisis of 1833.

In 1828, Congress passed a tariff designed to protect the northern industrial economy, which was struggling to compete against low cost imported goods. Southerners generally opposed the tariff because it raised the price of goods imported into southern states, goods they could not manufacture themselves. It also indirectly hurt the southern agrarian economy by reducing cash available for the English to purchase southern cotton. Opposition proved particularly fierce in South Carolina. Many southerners dubbed it the Tariff of Abominations.

Opponents claimed the tariff of 1828 was unconstitutional because it benefited only certain sections of the country to the detriment of others. In other words, they believed it represented an actual violation of the general welfare clause.

North Carolina issued a solemn protest in 1828, declaring, "Manufactures in the United States, are not an object of general interest, but of local interest..."

John Quincy Adams lost the presidential election later that year, and Andrew Jackson took up residence at the White House. Vice President John C. Calhoun, who retained his office in the 1828 election, vehemently opposed the tariff. In December 1828, he secretly wrote a pamphlet entitled South Carolina Exposition and Protest. He laid out the case against the tariff, arguing tariff power was only rightly used to raise revenue.

> *"The General Government is one of specific powers, and it can rightfully exercise only the powers expressly granted, and those that may be necessary and proper to carry them into effect, all others being reserved expressly to the States or the people. It results, necessarily, that those who claim to exercise power under the Constitution, are bound to show that it is expressly granted, or that it is necessary and proper as a means of the granted powers. The advocates of the Tariff have offered no such proof. It is true that the third section of the first article of the Constitution authorizes Congress to lay and collect an impost duty, but it is granted as a tax power for the sole purpose of revenue, a power in its nature essentially different from that of imposing protective or prohibitory duties. Their objects are incompatible. The prohibitory system must end in destroying the revenue from imports."*

And he argued South Carolina possessed the right and power to step in and nullify the tariff.

> *"If it be conceded, as it must be by every one who is the least conversant with our institutions, that the sovereign powers delegated are divided between the General and State Governments, and that the latter hold their portion by the same tenure as the former, it would seem impossible to deny to the States the right*

*of deciding on the infractions of their powers, and the
proper remedy to be applied for their correction. The
right of judging, in such cases, is an essential attribute
of sovereignty, of which the States cannot be divested
without losing their sovereignty itself, and being
reduced to a subordinate corporate condition."*

He concluded the pamphlet with a forceful call for the state to step
in.

*"With these views the committee are solemnly of the
impression, if the present usurpations and the
professed doctrines of the existing system be
persevered in, after due forebearance on the part of
the State, that it will be her sacred duty to interpose
her veto; duty to herself, to the Union, to the present,
and to future generations, arid to the cause of liberty
over the world, to arrest the progress of a usurpation
which, if not arrested, must, in its consequences,
corrupt the public morals and destroy the liberty of
the country."(4)*

The tariff's effect on the southern economy proved disastrous.
England predictably reduced its cotton imports, and southern states
were forced to purchase manufactured goods at higher prices from
northern U.S. manufacturers.

The relationship between Jackson and Calhoun deteriorated as the
president refused to address southern grievances. In 1832, Calhoun
resigned the vice presidency and filled an open seat in the Senate.

That same year, Congress passed the Tariff of 1832, but it did little to
relieve the burden on southern states. In response, South Carolina
elected delegates to a special convention and on Nov. 24, the
convention ratified the South Carolina Ordinance of Nullification. The
proclamation declared the tariffs of 1828 and 1832, "are
unauthorized by the constitution of the United States, and violate the

true meaning and intent thereof and are null, void, and no law, nor binding upon this State."(5)

The delegates set Feb. 1, 1833 as the date noncompliance would go into effect.

Jackson issued a strong response, forcefully challenging the legality of nullification and threatening to use force should South Carolina go forward and refuse to collect the tariff. In his address to Congress on Dec. 3, Jackson wrote:

> *"It is my painful duty to state that in one quarter of the United States opposition to the revenue laws has arisen to a height which threatens to thwart their execution, if not to endanger the integrity of the Union. What ever obstructions may be thrown in the way of the judicial authorities of the General Government, it is hoped they will be able peaceably to overcome them by the prudence of their own officers and the patriotism of the people. But should this reasonable reliance on the moderation and good sense of all portions of our fellow citizens be disappointed, it is believed that the laws themselves are fully adequate to the suppression of such attempts as may be immediately made. Should the exigency arise rendering the execution of the existing laws impracticable from any cause what ever, prompt notice of it will be given to Congress, with a suggestion of such views and measures as may be deemed necessary to meet it."(6)*

Eight days later, Jackson issued the Proclamation to the People of South Carolina, condemning nullification.

South Carolina refused to back down. The legislature responded with a resolution of its own, declaring, "The state will repel force by force, and relying on the blessings of God, will maintain its liberty at all hazards."(7)

Ultimately, Kentucky Senator Henry Clay diffused the situation, brokering a compromise that lowered the tariff over the next 10 years.

Conventional wisdom holds that South Carolina's decision to nullify the tariffs was a disaster and a failure. But was it? While proponents of nullification certainly can't claim total victory – the tariff did remain in place after all - South Carolina's efforts led to a shift in policy. The state did what Madison suggested and created "serious impediments," winning at least a partial victory.

Imagine the results if other southern states stood in solidarity with the Palmetto State.

Tom Woods sums it up in his book *Nullification: How to Resist Federal Tyranny in the 21st Century.*

> "South Carolina stared down the federal government and won for the South a program of tariff relief it might otherwise not have received. The compromise reached between the federal government and South Carolina demonstrates the value of nullification, not its fruitlessness."(8)

Was it messy?

Yes!

Was it a difficult and dangerous time?

Certainly!

But the process brought about needed change for southern states, and ultimately, the ends testify to the effectiveness of the means.

But many people fear messiness, and oftentimes, the desire for peace and security lead people to accept the dangers of centralized power.

In the aftermath of the nullification crisis, several states condemned nullification and South Carolina specifically for attempting to implement it. Even some southern states typically sympathetic to state sovereignty arguments piled on. Jackson biographer, Robert Remini, chronicles southern backlash against South Carolina.

> *"The Alabama legislature, for example, pronounced the doctrine 'unsound in theory and dangerous in practice.' Georgia said it was 'mischievous,' 'rash and revolutionary.' Mississippi lawmakers chided the South Carolinians for acting with 'reckless precipitancy.'"*(9)

Even James Madison opposed South Carolina nullification. One of the architects of the doctrine suddenly reversed course, arguing a single state does not have the power to nullify a federal law. Of course, this represents a shift in position. A careful reading of the Virginia Resolution of 1798 and the Virginia Report of 1800 makes it clear Madison absolutely believed a single state should and could interpose to "arrest the progress of evil" and to protect authorities, liberties and rights, "within their respective limits," i.e. state borders. Reading Madison's letters on the subject, two things become clear. He thought the tariff was a mistake, but not unconstitutional, and he vehemently advocated for preserving the Union, viewing South Carolina's response as a legitimate threat to it.

It's also important to note that Madison's objection was directed toward a particular scheme concocted by South Carolina based on the general nullification principle. Madison explains the focus of his objections in his *1835 Notes on Nullification.*

> *"That the doctrine of nullification may be clearly understood it must be taken as laid down in the Report of a special committee of the House of Representatives of S. C. in 1828. In that document it is asserted, that a single State has a constitutional right to arrest the execution of a law of the U. S. within its limits; that the arrest is to be presumed right and valid, and is to remain in force unless ¾ of the States, in a Convention, shall otherwise decide."* (10)

In essence, the South Carolina nullifying scheme asserted a single state had the Constitutional power to dictate the actions of the other states. The Palmetto State claimed that the entire Union must recognize its nullifying efforts; that a single state had veto power over any federal act and its nullifying act bound every other state until the states called conventions and voted otherwise. The assertion made by South Carolina was really a bastardization of the actual principle of nullification. Madison rightly argues that, no, a state does not have this kind of constitutional authority.

But opponents of nullification should also be aware that Madison never completely backed away from the Principles of '98. Even in his letters during the tariff crisis in the 1830s, he admitted the validity of nullification after states exhausted all other constitutional remedies.

> "She (Virginia in the 1798 Resolutions) asserted moreover & offered her proofs that the States had a right in such cases, to interpose, first in their constituent character to which the govt of the U. S. was responsible, and otherwise as specially provided by the Constitution; and further, that the States, in their capacity of parties to and creators of the Constitution, had an ulterior right to interpose, notwithstanding any decision of a constituted authority; which, however it might be the last resort under the forms of the Constitution in cases falling within the scope of its functions, could not preclude an interposition of the States as the parties which made the Constitution and, as such, possessed an authority paramount to it."(11)

It remains unclear why Madison created this convoluted argument, asserting that states could nullify, but a single state can't, but then again it can if it must, turning his back on the clear language of the Virginia Resolutions instead of simply saying, "I stand by what I said in 1798, but it doesn't apply now." He even went as far as to claim Jefferson never used the word nullification. He had to back off that one after someone showed him an original draft of Jefferson's Kentucky Resolutions.

While I'm only speculating, it seems the backlash against the Principles of '98 in the wake of the nullification crisis had more to do with weariness, wariness and a strong desire to preserve the Union, rather than an actual philosophical opposition to nullification. Perhaps this explains Madison's apparent lukewarm attachment late in life to the idea he helped formulate. Perhaps his fear of schism led him to back far away from the idea, hoping to douse smoldering embers. Or maybe Madison simply flip-flopped. He certainly wouldn't be the first politician to do so.

Regardless of Madison's motives, the nullification fight clearly stirred up emotions across the U.S., and many undoubtedly believed a major disaster was narrowly averted. The nullification idea went dormant for a short time, and with a tariff compromise reached, nobody seemed much inclined to push the issue any further. The echoes of saber rattling still resonated across the United States, and the fatigue of conflict and the raw emotions left in the aftermath of a debate that brought the U.S. and South Carolina to the brink of open warfare certainly didn't create an environment conducive to a continued ideological battle. Sometimes it's easier to go along to get along.

But regardless of whether or not you agree that the tariff represented a valid reason for South Carolina to assert its right to nullify, it ultimately worked to some degree, messy and dangerous though it was.

When it comes down to it, many Americans simply don't have the spine or fortitude to stand up and fight, even with liberty on the line. But self-government requires the people to engage and take action. Otherwise, the system begins to run on its own accord, growing ever larger, more powerful and less responsive to those it was meant to serve. Soon, the servant becomes the master. The Marshmallow Man grows ever larger, soon wrapping his sticky arms around everything. Sometimes, we have to stand up, take the role of Ghostbuster, and cut the monster back down to size. It's hard. It's messy. And sometimes, it's downright scary. But stand up we must. The alternative looks far bleaker than the risk of conflict.

In truth, some things must count as worth fighting for.

Just a few years later, northern abolitionists found their own cause, reawakening the desire to fight, and they too appealed to the Principles of '98.

6

NULLIFICATION: NOT JUST FOR RACISTS ANYMORE. NEVER WAS.

Imagine a zombie conducting a television interview with the author of a book on nullification. Naturally the undead can only utter one word at a time. He holds up the book, speaking in a drawn out monotone, and declares, "Booook."

The enthusiastic writer eagerly explains the premise of his work, only to have the zombie declare, "Raaaacist."

"No, no," the author replies, going on to explain the very non-racist applications of nullification. Unconvinced, the zombie points accusingly, "Neooo-confederate."

And on it goes.

Thomas Woods produced a hilarious video along these lines shortly after the release of his book, *Nullification: How to Resist Tyranny in the 21st Century.*"(1)

Start a conversation about nullification and you will likely find yourself treated in much the same way our undead journalist treated

Woods in his video. Nullification opponents may find it difficult to refute the historical or philosophical basis of the principle, but allegations of racism flow easily over their lips, like sweet tea from a frosty glass on a hot summer Birmingham day. Listen closely to the undertones in most arguments against nullification, and you will likely come away with the impression that everybody advancing the idea flies the Stars and Bars in their front yard, stores grey uniforms in their closets and longs for the day when the South will finally rise again.

On April 12, 2011, MSNBC commentator Rachel Maddow put together a segment on nullification called *Confederates in the Attic*.(2) She masterfully tied the Principles of '98 to slavery, choosing the 150th anniversary of the opening shots of the Civil War at Fort Sumter to air her missive.

Early in the piece, a full-screen sketch of John C. Calhoun appears.

> "The great pride of the South Carolina secessionists was this guy, this guy with the teen-idol good looks, Sen. John C. Calhoun, the beloved pro-slavery politician who was South Carolina's greatest political export at that time," she intones. "As well as being a rabid proponent of slavery, John Calhoun, to that end, championed the cause of nullification."

As we discussed in the last chapter, Calhoun did indeed support the doctrine of nullification, and he articulately defended it. But slavery wasn't the issue. Calhoun advocated for nullification in opposition to the Tariff of Abominations, some 30 years before the War Between the States. Still, Maddow can't resist the temptation to tie Calhoun's support for slavery to his defense of nullification. Of course, she never points out that his most fierce opponent during the nullification crisis was also a pro-slavery Southern Democrat, President Andrew Jackson. By her logic, those opposing nullification must also do so with racist intent, right?

Oblivious to her own historical ignorance, Maddow plunges on.

> "But it's not only fighting over what happened back then. What is remarkable 150 years after the start of the Civil War is how right now – now – so many of the hallmarks of the Civil War and of the Confederacy are in political fashion again. Nullification, which helped steer South Carolina into its militant, anti-U.S. stance – nullification is now enjoying a remarkable renaissance."

She cannot refute nullification on a historical or philosophical basis, so Maddow meanders down the well-worn path traveled by so many nullification opponents - to the elementary school playground. Unable to compete based on facts, reason or logic; she simply calls her opponent names.

The race card slap-down becomes even more pathetic considering Maddow and her like-minded central government supporters twist history 180 degrees the wrong way.

Fact: Southerners never utilized nullification in support of slavery. Slavery was the law of the land, the official policy of the federal government. What exactly did supporters of slavery have to nullify?

In fact, it was northern abolitionists who appealed to the principles of nullification to oppose fugitive slave laws. Ironically, abolitionists often invoked Calhoun's arguments to support their position. (3)

The state convention convened by South Carolina to consider secession wrote a *Declaration of the Immediate Causes Which Induce and Justify the Secession of South Carolina from the Federal Union*. One of the chief complaints: northern state nullification.

> *"An increasing hostility on the part of the non-slaveholding States to the institution of slavery, has led to a disregard of their obligations, and the laws of the General Government have ceased to effect the*

*objects of the Constitution. The States of Maine, New
Hampshire, Vermont, Massachusetts, Connecticut,
Rhode Island, New York, Pennsylvania, Illinois,
Indiana, Michigan, Wisconsin and Iowa, have enacted
laws which either nullify the Acts of Congress or
render useless any attempt to execute them."*(4)

The acts of Congress they referred to: the Fugitive Slave Act
of 1850.

The Constitution did provide for the return of runaway slaves to their
"owners."

> *"No Person held to Service or Labour in one State,
> under the Laws thereof, escaping into another, shall,
> in Consequence of any Law or Regulation therein, be
> discharged from such Service or Labour, But shall be
> delivered up on Claim of the Party to whom such
> Service or Labour may be due." – Article IV, Sec. 2*

But many in northern states contended that the fugitive-slave laws
passed by Congress in support of the constitutional provision violated
important constitutional principles, particularly the most draconian
Fugitive Slave Act of 1850. For instance, the 1850 act made a farce of
due process, allowing for the arrest of a suspected runaway slave
based on the word of the "property owner." He simply had to swear
an affidavit attesting to his "ownership" of the person in question.

> *"In no trial or hearing under this act shall the
> testimony of such alleged fugitive be admitted in
> evidence; and the certificates in this and the first
> [fourth] section mentioned, shall be* **conclusive** *of the
> right of the person or persons in whose favor granted,
> to remove such fugitive to the State or Territory from
> which he escaped, and shall prevent all molestation of
> such person or persons by any process issued by any*

*court, judge, magistrate, or other person
whomsoever." (Emphasis added)(5)*

Abolitionists, and even many average northerners, considered actions taken under the Fugitive Slave Act akin to sanctioned kidnapping.

The Fugitive Slave Act of 1850 also obligated citizens of free states to serve as slave catchers, empowering commissioners appointed to capture runaway slaves to, "to summon and call to their aid the bystanders, or posse comitatus of the proper county, when necessary to ensure a faithful observance of the clause of the Constitution referred to, in conformity with the provisions of this act; and all good citizens are hereby commanded to aid and assist in the prompt and efficient execution of this law, whenever their services may be required, as aforesaid, for that purpose; and said warrants shall run, and be executed by said officers, any where in the State within which they are issued."

Additionally, the law provided that fugitive-slave commissioners receive pay based on fees – in essence a bounty. Commissioners received $10 for returning an alleged slave to an "owner," only $5, "in cases where the proof shall not, in the opinion of such commissioner, warrant such certificate and delivery..."

The Constitution requires fixed salaries for judicial officers, rendering this provision unconstitutional.

Instead of simply submitting to federal authority and quietly participating in constitutionally dubious and morally reprehensible fugitive-slave roundups, northerners aggressively resisted the fugitive slave acts. Officials in these states did everything within their power to thwart enforcement of the acts, including denying federal agents the use of jails, and even impeaching state officials who lent support to fugitive-slave claimants.

Keep in mind, the U.S. Supreme Court ruled early versions of these personal liberty laws unconstitutional in Prigg v. Pennsylvania (1842).

Some states backed off at that point, and simply passed acts prohibiting state cooperation in fugitive slave hunting. This forced slave commissioners to kidnap suspected runaways, making them a target for criminal prosecution under state kidnapping laws.

And when Congress passed the even more aggressive Fugitive Slave Act of 1850, northern states gave the Supreme Court the proverbial finger and passed aggressive "Liberty Laws." For instance, in 1855 the Massachusetts legislature passed a law called, *An Act to Protect the Rights and Liberties of the People of the Commonwealth of Massachusetts*. A key provision called for the removal of any state official who aided in the return of runaway slaves. Another section authorized impeachment of state judges who accepted federal commissioner positions authorizing them to prosecuted fugitive slaves.

> *"Any person holding any judicial office under the constitution or laws of this Commonwealth, who shall continue, for ten days after the passage of this act, to hold the office of United States commissioner, or any office...which qualifies him to issue any warrant or other process...under the [Fugitive Slave Acts] shall be deemed to have violated good behavior, to have given reason for the loss of public confidence, and furnished sufficient ground either for impeachment or for removal by address." (6)*

A Michigan act passed in 1855 denied the use of state or local jails for holding suspected runaway slaves and guaranteed any accused fugitive slave a jury trial.

> *"All persons so arrested and claimed as fugitive slaves, shall be entitled to all the benefits of the writ of habeas corpus and of trial by jury."(7)*

So for all of her rhetorical and visual gymnastics, Maddow gets it wrong. Nullification has nothing to do with slavery and oppression.

Nullification is all about freedom and liberty.

Nothing more vividly illustrates this truth than the story of Joshua Glover.(8)

We know little about the first 36 years of Joshua's life. We don't know where he was born, who his parents where, or whether he had any brothers or sisters. At this point in the story, we don't even know his last name. You see, slaves didn't get last names. To endow a man with a last name humanizes him. The institution of slavery would never have survived as long as it did if people allowed themselves to view slaves as fellow human beings.

We may not know where Joshua spent the first 36 years of his life, but we do know where he spent New Year's Eve 1849. While other St. Louis residents celebrated the coming of the New Year, Joshua sat in a pen waiting for the following day's slave sale. A preacher visited one of the St. Louis slave pens operated by a prominent slave trader named Bernard Lynch and described the horrendous conditions. Really a private jail, the small cramped room featured a dirt floor. A single window high up on the wall afforded the only light. The room was furnished with three wooden, backless benches. Men and women shared the space with no provision for privacy. In a St. Louis newspaper ad, Lynch boasted he provided "a good yard for their accommodation and comfortable quarters under secure fastening."

The following morning, handlers marched Joshua outside, naked, into the winter chill. Prominent citizens arrived from all over the state, seeking the opportunity to purchase a slave. It was more than a financial transaction. Slave ownership indicated high social standing, and prospective buyers, dressed in their finest, hitched their best horses to their nicest wagons and made their way into downtown St. Louis. It was partly business trip, partly an opportunity to see and be seen.

The auctioneer and his assistants offered slaves for inspection prior to bidding. Prospective buyers moved from person to person, poking and prodding, looking for signs of strength or ill health. An astute slaveholder paid particular attention to a slaves back, looking for whip marks that would indicate a misbehaving slave. It apparently never crossed their minds that excessive whipping could indicate a "bad master." A prospective owner went as far as to pry open a man's mouth to inspect his teeth, much like an experienced groom examines the teeth of a race horse. They were not only looking for signs of health, but also for "blue gum n-." A rampant superstition throughout the South held that the bite of a black man with blue gums was more deadly than a rattlesnake.

As if the indignity of another man inspecting him like a piece of merchandise wasn't enough, the auctioneer expected the slave to sell himself to perspective buyers. This created something of a double-edged sword. Boast too much about your strength and productivity and your new master would likely punish you severely when he discovered you weren't up to par. But undersell yourself, and you might receive a beating on the spot. So the slave walked a fine line, talking himself up enough to satisfy the seller, but not so much as to create unreasonable expectations in the mind of the buyer.

The prospective slave owners wandering among the Negroes on the steps of the St. Louis courthouse that New Year's Day in 1850 found no marks on Glover's back. In fact, he was known as a hard worker. And strong. He stood between 5-foot-8 and 5-foot-10 with a slender build. He had long legs for a man his height, with large feet and hands, and a bushy head of hair.

One of the men looking to buy that day was Benammi Stone Garland. Originally from Lynchburg, Virginia, he was a prominent farmer, owning a large 300 acre spread about four miles west of St. Louis. Records indicate Garland grew hay, oats, corn, potatoes and ran dairy cattle. The farm also featured an orchard. According to tax records, the farm was valued at around $60,000, quite a sum in those days.

It wasn't Garland's first trip to the slave auctions. He already owned three males, ages 18, 16 and 15, along with a 36-year-old woman and a 9-year-old girl, who likely served in a domestic capacity. When Garland left St. Louis that day, he owned his sixth human being – Joshua.

For the next two years, Joshua labored. He worked sunup to sundown, sometimes longer. And the labor wasn't easy. If you've ever worked on a farm, you know. Joshua didn't get sick days or holidays. He didn't stay inside when it snowed or rained, or when the temperatures dropped well below freezing. Choice did not make up any part of his day-to-day existence. He did what he was told when he was told to do it. No questions asked.

From our perspective, it's hard to imagine NOT contemplating escape. We look at the life Joshua was subjected to and think, "Hell no! I would never accept that." But stop and reconsider – it was the only life he ever knew. And while he lacked freedom and creature comforts, he had food to eat, a circle of friends and a daily routine. Face it – we generally embrace our routine, despite the drudgery it may entail, and we tend to fear the unknown. We accept the evil we know over the evil we don't know. On top of that, take into account the risk that came with escape. If caught, the runaway slave faced, at best, a severe beating. Or the owner might just "sell him south." That would mean living under even harsher conditions on plantations in Mississippi or Louisiana. Or the worst case scenario – death. There was little to stop an owner from killing a wayward slave.

But at some point, Joshua decided that freedom was worth the risk. We will never know what prompted him to make the break. Perhaps it was a particular incident. Or maybe it was just the accumulated weight of a life of slavery.

In May of 1852, Joshua made his move. Garland's farm was located within about five miles of the Mississippi River. Alton, Ill., a town known for its abolitionist sympathies, nestled along the opposite bank. Moored in the river between St. Louis and her sister city, a barge used as a school for black children. It also served as an avenue of escape. On that May night, Joshua snuck onto the barge, and under the cover of darkness it was moved over to the Illinois side of the river. When Joshua set foot on the opposite bank, he took his first step as a free man.

We don't know what went through his mind as he stood there on free soil for the first time in his life. It's not hard to imagine that he looked up into the dark, night sky and uttered a prayer of thanksgiving. But this only marked the beginning of a long, tedious journey. For the next six to seven weeks, Joshua walked. With only the clothes on his back and a few meager possessions, he trekked more than 350 miles. He traveled mostly at night, guided by the North Star. Slaves knew to use the Big Dipper, referred to as the Drinkin' Gourd, to locate the North Star and navigate. His hunger kept him company. He apparently took little with him and scavenged for food. Joshua later said a kind woman gave him a few seed potatoes. At one point, he went three days with nothing at all to eat.

Ultimately, Joshua chose to set down roots in Racine, Wis. We don't have any indication as to why he finally stopped in Racine, a town on the Root River, about 25 miles from Milwaukee. He might have heard of the strong anti-slavery sentiment there. Perhaps he just got tired of walking. The town had a small black population, and Joshua likely got information from the locals about who to trust, where to find work and how generally to get by in the small frontier town of about 500 residents. A mill owner named Justin Sinclair hired Joshua. He received a small salary, and the mill provided a place to live, with rent deducted from his wages. His home was really little more than a shanty. But it was his shanty. Granted, he still worked long hard hours, but at the end of the week, he received a wage for his labor.

He also took a last name: Glover.

Joshua Glover was a free man.

Glover lived and worked in Racine peacefully for about two years. But he was always looking over his shoulder. Despite living on free soil, every former slave knew their previous "owner" could roll into town demanding the return of their "property." And slave catchers roamed the northern states, collecting a bounty for dragging men back into servitude. Even free blacks lived under a cloud, because it only took the word of a white man to establish ownership. More than one legitimately free black found himself dragged south into slavery on the word of a lying slave-owner or a greedy commissioner.

And Garland wasn't one to let his property go without a fight. Shortly after Glover escaped, Garland ran an ad in the Missouri Republican offering a $200 reward.

> *"Ran away from the subscriber, living four miles west of the city of St. Louis on Saturday night last, a negro man by the name of Joshua; about 35 or 40 years of age, about 6 feet high, spare, with long legs and short body, full suit of hair, eyes inflamed and red; his color is an ashy black. Had on when he left away a pair of black satinet pantaloons, pair of heavy kip boots, an old-fashioned black dress coat, and osnaburg shirt. He took no clothes with him. The above reward will be paid for his apprehension if taken out of the State, and fifty dollars if taken in the State."*

> *B.S. Garland, May 17, 1852*

Ultimately, Garland tracked down Glover in Racine, likely with the help of another former slave named Nelson Turner. Turner hailed from Natchez, Miss. and befriended Glover in Racine. Apparently, Turner valued a little cash more than freedom or friendship. Historians believe he made at least two trips to St. Louis during the winter to consult with Garland. In March of 1854, Garland executed an affidavit attesting to his ownership of Glover and presented it to Andrew G. Miller, a federal judge in Milwaukee. The judge issued an order for Joshua's arrest, and Garland put together a posse, led by Deputy U.S. Marshal Charles C. Cotton.

On March 10, the posse rolled up into the yard in front of Glover's shanty. Inside, Glover played cards and drank a little whiskey with Nelson and another man. Joshua reportedly drank sparingly. He was likely nervous about news of slave catchers in the area. There were also rumors that Glover was "romancing" Nelson's wife and didn't quite trust his "friend's" intentions. This fact could also account for the former Mississippi slave's willingness to sell out a fellow freedman.

Suddenly, a banging on the door.

"Don't open it 'til we know who's there!" Glover screamed.

Too late.

Nelson leapt up and flung the door open. Garland, Cotton and the rest of the posse stormed inside. Garland barged in armed with a pistol, and Glover tried to wrest it from his former "owner's" hand. But before Joshua could gain control of the weapon, Cotton cracked him over the head with a pair of handcuffs. Another man struck Glover with the butt of a whip, and the former slave fell to his dirt floor, dazed and bleeding profusely. The posse manacled Glover, dragged him from his home and tossed him like a sack into the back of a waiting wagon, his bleeding head between his "master's" knees.

With Glover in custody, Garland and his posse elected to make the 25 mile trip to Milwaukee and lodge Joshua in jail there overnight. They apparently felt the Racine jail too vulnerable and probably knew the general population wouldn't react well to a gang of men dragging one of their fellow citizens out of his own home.

On that count, they were correct.

Word got out quickly. That same night, Charles Rice, Glover's employer at the mill, rode into town and reported to Charles

Clement, the abolitionist editor of the Racine Advocate, that Glover had been "kidnapped" and taken to Milwaukee. Clement wrote up a short article for the Saturday morning paper and then telegraphed Sherman Booth, the editor of the Milwaukee Free Democrat.

Early the next morning, Booth set about gathering facts. It proved difficult. Cotton lied to the newspaperman, denying any knowledge of the event. Judge Miller also refused to divulge much information, although Booth did confirm an arrest warrant was issued for a runaway slave two days earlier. Booth finally learned Glover was in the county jail from the father of a local lawyer.

Booth went back to his office and typed up a handbill.

MAN CAPTURED
OUR JAIL USED FOR THE SLAVE-CATCHERS!

Last night a colored man was arrested near Racine, on a warrant of Judge Miller by Deputy Sheriff Cotton and making some resistance, was knocked down and brought to this City, and incarcerated in the County Jail. Marshal Cotton denied knowing anything about it at 9 o'clock this morning. The object evidently is to get him a secret trial without giving him a chance to defend himself by counsel. Citizens of Milwaukee! Shall we have Star Chamber proceedings here? And shall a man be dragged back to Slavery from our Free Soil, without an open trial of his right to Liberty? Watch your jail, your District and U.S. Commissioners' Courts!
Milwaukee, March 11, 1854

That morning in Racine, bells chimed, and the largest crowd in town history gathered in the square. A committee quickly organized. It formulated demands, including a fair and impartial jury trial for Glover. The local authorities also issued warrants for Garland and Cotton's arrest on assault charges. The town selected a group of 100 delegates to go with the sheriff to Milwaukee, and bring Cotton and Garland back to Racine to face charges. That represented no small decision lightly considered. It flew square in the face of federal law.

Those electing to go out and attempt arresting a federal agent risked imprisonment themselves.

Meanwhile, a large crowd gathered in front of the county jail in Milwaukee. Booth rode his horse through town announcing, "Free citizens who do not wish to be made slaves or slave-catchers, meet at the Courthouse Square at 2 o'clock." By 2:30 p.m., between 3,000 and 5,000 people filled the square. Speakers condemning slavery in general, and Glover's jailing in particular, fired up the crowd. City officials called in the militia and fire companies to control the gathering, but only one company of 40 men even answered the call. They quickly disbanded seeing the large agitated crowd.

At about 5 p.m., the contingent from Racine showed up. As they arrived, a local attorney with strong abolitionist leaning named Charles K. Watkins spoke, telling the crowd that sometimes people had to take the law into their own hands or risk becoming slaves themselves. Tensions ran high as Booth spoke next. Finally, it snapped like an overextended rubber band. The crowd began to press toward the jail. Some kicked down an outer door. Others used a pickaxe to knock down a wall near the guard door. People began demanding keys to the jail. A mason by the name of James Angrove picked up a six inch diameter beam from a nearby construction sight and yelled, "Here's a good enough key!" Several people grabbed the makeshift battering ram and bludgeoned down the jail door. Those nearby reportedly heard Glover cry, "Hallelujah!" and moments later he emerged from the jail, waving his hat at the crowd as he left.

Reports say that town folk reacted as if it were the Fourth of July. Reports described Glover's escape as part flight, part parade. His rescuers ushered him into a two-horse wagon, and the procession slowly made its way out of town. People pressed in to touch Joshua and shake his hand as he passed by. When the procession reached Walker's Point Bridge, Glover transferred into a lighter, speedier one-horse wagon owned by a man named John Messenger.

Messenger didn't have a reputation as an activist and apparently just got caught up in the events of the day. In fact, the well-known building contractor was described as a, "rabid Democrat changed in a night to a rank abolitionist." He risked his own reputation, income, family and even his own freedom to drive Glover 16 miles west, in near freezing temperatures, to a town called Waukesha. There, Messenger delivered Joshua to the home of Winchel D. Bacon, a safe-house along the famed Underground Railroad.

Over the next two weeks, Glover moved from house to house along the Underground Railroad. He traveled some 100 miles and made seven stops, ultimately ending up in Spring Prairie, a mere 20 miles from his home in Racine. After several more weeks, and another three moves, Joshua holed up in the warehouse of Dutton and Raymond in Racine. From there, he snuck onto a Canadian bound steamer for the final leg of his journey to freedom. He hid in the cargo hold during the trip, with only a bucket for a toilet, depending on the kindness of others to bring him food. The trip generally took three to four days, that is, if conditions were good.

Ultimately, Joshua Glover found the freedom he so desperately yearned for. On April 19, we find the first evidence of Glover's presence in Etobikoke, Ontario, a village a short distance from Toronto. He took a job at an inn owned by a man named Thomas Montgomery and worked there the rest of his life. Records show he labored for wages, earning about $2 a month, and he also grew his own food. Glover lived in a single story home, complete with a cook-stove. In 1861, he showed up on census records married to Ann Glover, an Irish woman. They remained married for 12 years, until her death.

Joshua died a free man on June 4, 1888, at around the age of 74.

Glover's freedom came at a price. Hundreds of people risked their own lives, liberty and property to earn a former slave the opportunity to live out his life as a truly free man. And several people paid dearly for their efforts.

John Messenger was reportedly "overwhelmed with anxiety" before he even returned to Milwaukee. He drove to Racine to stay with friends that night. They say he paced the floor and refused to eat or drink. His fears weren't unfounded. In April, Garland served Messenger with civil suit for $2,000, charging him with aiding the escape of a slave. And in July, the feds indicted him, along with Booth and another man, on criminal charges. Officers arrested Messenger on Aug. 2, and he posted bail. Two days later, he was dead. Historians have not been able to locate a death certificate and speculate he died from "other than natural causes," most likely suicide.

Sherman Booth found himself embroiled in legal wrangling for the next seven years. Authorities arrested him and brought him before a federal judge. When he applied for a writ of habeas corpus, a Wisconsin Supreme Court judge ordered Booth released, declaring the Fugitive Slave Act unconstitutional and therefore null and void in the state of Wisconsin. Federal agents later arrested Booth again. He was tried and found guilty of violating the Fugitive Slave Act. A federal judge sentenced him to one month in jail and fined him $1,000. The Wisconsin Supreme Court once again ordered Booth released and would not cooperate with the U.S. Supreme Court during appeal, refusing to send a proper record of the case to Washington D.C. That delayed further action until March 1857. In 1858, the U.S. Supreme Court ordered Booth into federal custody. The state refused to comply yet again.

The Wisconsin legislature supported and affirmed the actions of the state Supreme Court. On March 19, 1859, the legislature passed the following resolution.

Whereas, The Supreme Court of the United States has assumed appellate jurisdiction in the matter of the petition of Sherman M. Booth for a writ of habeas corpus, presented and prosecuted to final judgment in the Supreme Court of this State, and has, without process, or any of the forms recognized by law, assumed the power to reverse that judgment in a matter involving the personal liberty of the citizen, asserted by and adjusted to him by the regular course of judicial proceedings upon the great writ of liberty secured to the people of each State by the Constitution of the United States:

And, whereas, Such assumption of power and authority by the Supreme Court of the United States, to become the final arbiter of the liberty of the citizen, and to override and nullify the judgments of the state courts' declaration thereof, is in a direct conflict with that provision of the Constitution of the United States which secures to the people the benefits of the writ of habeas corpus: therefore,

Resolved, The Senate concurring, That we regard the action of the Supreme Court of the United States, in assuming jurisdiction in the case before mentioned, as an arbitrary act of power, unauthorized by the Constitution, and virtually superseding the benefit of the writ of habeas corpus and prostrating the rights and liberties of the people at the foot of unlimited power.

Resolved, That this assumption of jurisdiction by the federal judiciary, in the said case, and without process, is an act of undelegated power, and therefore without authority, void, and of no force.

Resolved, That the government, formed by the Constitution of the United States was not the exclusive or final judge of the extent of the powers delegated to itself; but that, as in all other cases of compact among parties having no common judge, each party has an equal right to judge for itself, as well of infractions as of the mode and measure of redress.

Resolved, That the principle and construction contended for by the party which now rules in the councils of the nation, that the general government is the exclusive judge of the extent of the powers delegated to it, stop nothing short of despotism, since the discretion of those who administer the government, and not the Constitution, would be the measure of their powers; that the several states which formed that instrument, being sovereign and independent, have the unquestionable right to judge of its infraction; and that a positive defiance of those sovereignties, of all unauthorized acts done or attempted to be done under color of that instrument, is the rightful remedy.

A United States marshal ultimately captured Booth and jailed him on March 1, 1860. On Aug. 1, supporters "rescued" him from the jail. His freedom proved relatively short-lived. The feds re-arrested him Oct. 8, and he spent the next year-plus in prison. His jail-time extended far beyond his one-month sentence because he either could not, or refused to pay his fine.

Booth also lost a second civil court case, after the first resulted in a hung jury. In the second go-around, a jury granted Garland a $1,000 award plus $246 in court costs. It took Garland nearly a year and a half to collect. Finally, a U.S. Marshal directed Booth's printing press sold to satisfy the judgment.

Either unable or unwilling to pay his criminal fine, Booth remained in federal prison beyond his one-month sentence. Friends finally convinced him to appeal to President Buchanan for a pardon. But his request proved anything but repentant. Booth used the opportunity to write a blistering defense of his actions, calling his sentence "unjust and illegal," and his imprisonment "an outrage on my rights, and the rights of a sovereign state."

Unsurprisingly, U.S. Attorney General Jeremiah S. Black sent a letter back denying the appeal, and Booth remained in prison for another year. On March 2, 1861, the eve of Abraham Lincoln's inauguration, Buchanan granted a remission of the fine and costs, and freed Booth from prison.

Glover's yearning for freedom gave him the courage to strike out and seek it. He risked his very life for the basic right to determine his own fate. But the former slave would have never lived out the final years of his life as a free man where it not for the principled actions of Booth, Merchant and many other men and women along the Underground Railroad who risked their own lives, limbs and fortunes for the principles of liberty. These woman and men literally bought his freedom, paying a price through their efforts. The cost proved steep, but they refused to simply submit to an immoral and unwarranted exercise of power over the rights of a fellow human being.

It is upon these noble principles that nullification rest: as Jefferson put it in the Kentucky Resolution of 1798, "on the belief that the several States composing the United States of America are not united on the principle of unlimited submission to their general government." We don't simply give in to tyranny because the federal government wields more power.

We fight.

On Dec. 1, 1955, Rosa Parks refused to give in.

When the white only seats in the front of the Cleveland Avenue bus in Montgomery, Ala. filled with passengers, leaving several white men standing, bus driver James Blake moved the "colored" section sign behind the row Parks was sitting in and demanded that she and the three other people move to seats in the rear of the bus.

The three other people in the row complied. Parks did not.

"When he saw me still sitting, he asked if I was going to stand up, and I said, 'No, I'm not.' And he said, 'Well, if you don't stand up, I'm going to have to call the police and have you arrested.' I said, 'You may do that,'" Parks recalled in a 1987 PBS documentary on the Civil Rights movement.(9)

Blake called the police and an officer arrested Parks. She spent the next day in jail. She was tried four days later and convicted of disorderly conduct. The judge fined her $10 and $4 in court costs. She also lost her job as a seamstress at a local department store.

"People always say that I didn't give up my seat because I was tired, but that isn't true. I was not tired physically, or no more tired than I usually was at the end of a working day. I was not old, although some people have an image of me as being old then. I was forty-two. No, the only tired I was, was tired of giving in," she wrote in her autobiography.(10)

She refused to submit.

Frederick Douglass was another man who knew the horror of slavery and longed for freedom. He too recognized the horror of unlimited submission.

> "Find out just what the people will submit to and you have found out the exact amount of injustice and wrong which will be imposed upon them; and these will continue until they are resisted with either words or blows, or with both. The limits of tyrants are prescribed by the endurance of those whom they oppress."

Nullification isn't just for racists anymore. In fact, it never was. Nullification is about reining in an overreaching, ever growing federal government and corralling it within its constitutionally defined sphere.

Without a doubt, racists appealed to state sovereignty and nullification, and state governments advanced "states' rights" arguments to justify trampling on the civil rights of black Americans during the 1940s, 50s and 60s. But those who point these facts out to discredit state sovereignty and nullification make a fallacious argument. The fact that some evil people turned to these principles to perpetuate an evil system of Jim Crow laws doesn't negate their legitimacy and value, any more than a crazed lunatic wielding a hammer, committing murder, makes the hammer itself an evil tool. Hammers still come in pretty handy for driving nails. And as we've seen, nullification has primarily been advanced to promote freedom, liberty and justice.

Certainly, the United States federal government serves as a force for good on occasion. But as we say in Kentucky, "Even a blind squirrel finds a nut every now and again." Historically, the vast majority of atrocities perpetrated through history find their roots in highly centralized power structures.

Generally speaking, bigger is badder.

7

BIGGER IS BADDER

Supposed to keep from eroding.
Up telephone poles,
Which rear, half out of leafage
As though they would shriek,
Like things smothered by their own

Green, mindless, unkillable ghosts.
In Georgia, the legend says
That you must close your windows
At night to keep it out of the house.

The glass is tinged with green, even so,
As the tendrils crawl over the fields.

-From the poem Kudzu, by James Dickey

Anybody spending any time in the south knows all about Kudzu. The vine covers pretty much everything along some stretches of roadway in Georgia, Alabama and other southeastern states. Trees. Telephone poles. Abandoned cars.

Originally introduced to the U.S. during the Centennial Exposition in Philadelphia in 1876, the fast growing vine quickly became popular. Japanese exhibitors planted a garden of Kudzu during the expo, and Americans were drawn to the large green leaves and fragrant blooms.

During the Great Depression, the Soil Conservation Service promoted Kudzu for soil erosion control. Soon, Civilian Conservation Corps workers spread out across the southeast planting Kudzu. In the early 1940s, the government offered up to $8 an acre to farmers as an incentive to plant the vines in their fields. The hot humid climate proved ideal for the plant's growth, and Kudzu began a march across the south like Sherman's army. (1)

Turns out, it was a little too much of a good thing.

Kudzu grows as much as a foot a day. Soon it began to overgrow everything, squeezing out native plants, damaging the environment it was meant to protect.

Kind of like the federal government.

Sometimes, bigger is badder.

Americans instinctively distrust concentrated, centralized power. Doubt it? Go out on a busy sidewalk in any city and ask 10 people how they feel about corporate monopolies. Nine out of ten, if not all ten, will invariably condemn giant conglomerates. They will rail about unfair control of the market, express fear that monopolistic businesses will take advantage of the consumer and charge exorbitant prices, and approve of government action to prevent or break up monopolistic activity. Most Americans even express at least some distrust of generally respected companies like Microsoft – a business driving amazing technological advances in computing with astounding productivity benefits. When it comes to Monopoly, Americans may enjoy the board game, but almost all condemn the real thing.

Yet many of these same people won't bat an eye at monopolistic power vested in the U.S. federal government. In fact, they encourage it, calling for more and more agencies, performing more and more functions once left to state and local governments, or private organizations. This makes no sense. Government power presents a far greater threat to liberty and our way of life than an economic monopolist. After all, the government has guns. Walmart may screw you out of a few dollars on some made in China trinket. But the feds can throw you in prison if you defy their authority, and they hold the power to confiscate your money with the stroke of a pen.

Still, large numbers of Americans look to the federal government as the protector of liberty. Opponents of decentralization through principles such as state sovereignty and nullification almost always point to the Civil Rights movement as a great victory for centralized power, citing it as proof that we need the feds to safeguard Americans from tyrannical state governments. They invoke the specter of Jim Crow laws, recall images of Birmingham police firing water cannons at black people, and remind us that Arkansas Governor Orval Faubus ordered National Guard troops to block the entrance of Little Rock Central High School in order to keep nine African-American students out. But wrap your head around the illogical position these folks take. State governments threaten liberty. So, we need an even bigger, more powerful, centralized government to protect us? It's a little like insisting rescuers should pull a drowning man from a swimming pool and then toss him into the ocean in order to save his life.

During a Republican primary debate leading up to the 2012 presidential election, Sen. Rick Santorum (R-Pa.) illustrated this misplaced faith in the federal government as the "protector of the people." Like many Americans, he makes the erroneous assumption that Washington D.C. will protect the interests of its citizens, while state governments will trample rights and abuse its people. To hammer home his point, Santorum set the feds up as the defender of Americans against state government mass sterilization campaigns.

> "We have Ron Paul saying, 'Oh, whatever the states want to do under the Tenth Amendment is fine.' So if

the states want to pass polygamy, that's fine. If the states want to impose sterilization, that's fine. No! Our country is based on moral laws, ladies and gentleman. There are things the states can't do. Abraham Lincoln said, 'The states do not have the right to do wrong.' I respect the Tenth Amendment, but we are a nation that has values. We are a nation that was built on a moral enterprise. And states don't have the right to tramp over those because of the Tenth Amendment."(2)

In the first place, Santorum completely ignores the federalist system our founders created. The federal government was never intended to enforce a moral enterprise or exercise "police powers." That role was left to the states and the people. That's why you don't generally see the federal government enforcing murder or rape laws throughout the United States, only in Washington D.C. and other federal enclaves (per the "enclave clause" - AIS8C17). Beyond not understanding, or simply ignoring, the division of powers between state and federal governments in the American system, Santorum's comment reveals his misplaced faith in centralized power.

No government enjoys innate superiority over another. All governments operate subject to identical forces of human nature - a flawed nature that leads people to abuse power and seek their own self-interest if left unchecked.

Political philosopher Frederick Bastiat observed:

> *"But there is also another tendency that is common among people. When they can, they wish to live and prosper at the expense of others. This is no rash accusation. Nor does it come from a gloomy and uncharitable spirit. The annals of history bear witness to the truth of it: the incessant wars, mass migrations, religious persecutions, universal slavery, dishonesty in commerce and monopolies. This fatal desire has its origin in the very nature of man - - in that primitive, universal and insuppressible instinct that impels him to satisfy his desires with the least possible pain."*(3)

Apparently, Santorum assumes a mysterious substance sprinkled in the D.C. water supply makes federal officials more benevolent and moral than the men and women who frequent our 50 state capitols. Or perhaps mutations in the DNA of federal bureaucrats make them superior to state workers. Maybe he believes something in the air along the Potomac mystically negates basic human nature, rendering federal officials altruistic and dedicated to serving American citizens.

Or something.

A quote often attributed to George Washington sums up the danger of government power. ANY government power.

"Government is not reason; it is not eloquent; it is force. Like fire, it is a dangerous servant and a fearful master."

Even if the first president never uttered the words, they ring no less true.

And concentrated power poses an even greater danger. As Lord Acton observed, "Absolute power corrupts absolutely." When we step back and look at the nature of government, it becomes clear that placing all authority in Washington D.C. poses a much greater threat to the people than allowing state governments to exercise their powers individually.

Let's take Santorum's ridiculous assertion at face value. Let's say Kentucky passes a law mandating castration for every male over the age of 30. How long do you think it would take for the mass exodus to begin? Guaranteed, the population of males over the age of 30 in Tennessee, Ohio, Indiana, West Virginia and the other bordering states would skyrocket within hours of the passage of that legislation. And you'd likely find the guys that didn't care to leave the Bluegrass State gathered on the steps of the capitol in Frankfort, shotguns in hand.

But what would happen if the federal government passed such a law? Where would we go? How easy is it to leave the United States? What escape or recourse do we have? When the feds pass a law, we **all** get what we get.

Santorum supporters might assert, "Well, the federal government would never do such a thing." Really? Then why assume state governments would? And really, can you guarantee that? Have you ever heard of Tuskegee?

Between 1932 and 1972, the U.S. Public Health Service studied the unchecked progression of syphilis in poor black sharecroppers in Tuskegee, Ala. Officials told the subjects of these studies that they were receiving free government health care. Officials never told them they had syphilis, nor did doctors ever treat them for the disease. They were told their treatments were for "bad blood."(4) On the detestable scale, this ranks up near to top. Yet discussion of the Tuskegee experiments never includes stripping power from the federal government. In fact, the solution proposed, and ultimately implemented, was more federal government. Kind of like an extra dose of arsenic for the poisoning victim.

Thanks.

Here's a question for you. Why do we never hear the Tuskegee experiments invoked as a reason to distrust and limit federal power in the same way big government apologists use the Civil Rights era as a rational for growing the federal government and limiting the power of the states?

And another: if you can be so sure the federal government wouldn't pass Santorum's hypothetically created draconian sterilization law, how can you stand there with a straight face and argue that we need the federal government violating the Constitution to protect citizens from states passing such ridiculous legislation?

Fact: governments do bad things. All of them. Local governments. State governments. National governments. The question becomes, how can "we the people" best control them?

Clearly, citizens exercise more control over local and state governments. I know where my state representative works when not fulfilling his legislative duties. I can walk to his office in about 15 minutes, knock on his door and sit down and chat. I've done it before. And I know where he grocery shops. I chat with him on

Facebook on a regular basis. I used to babysit my state senator's kids. Tracking down my congressman plays out kind of like a real-life version of *Where's Waldo*. He excels at hiding from constituents. Everyday folks certainly can't just waltz into his office unannounced and expect him to hang out and shoot the breeze. And do you really think the president of the United States cares a wit about what average Joe or Jane thinks?

Thomas Woods asks the relevant question in his book, *Nullification: How to Resist Federal Tyranny in the 21st Century*.

"Is liberty more likely to be preserved under one monopoly jurisdiction, or through the competition of many jurisdictions?"(5)

The founders limited federal authority for a reason. They feared concentrated power. They had just fought a brutal, bloody war to escape the tyranny of unchecked power. The framers created a republican system with checks and balances, delegating a few specific roles to the general government, reserving the rest to the states and the people. As we discussed earlier in this book, not only did they create checks and balances within the federal system itself, they expected the states to serve as a check on federal power.

Virginia Judge Able P. Upshur explained the need for states to rein in federal power.

> "Power and patronage cannot easily be so limited and defined, as to rob them of their corrupting influences over the public mind. It is truly and wisely remarked in the Federalist that, "a power over a man's subsistence is a power over his will." As little as possible of this power should be entrusted to the federal government, and even that little should be watched by a power authorized and competent to arrest its abuses. That power can be found only in the States. In this consists the great superiority of the federative system over every other. In that system, the federal government is responsible, not directly to the people en masse, but to the people in their character of distinct political corporations. However

easy it may be to steal power from the people,
governments do not so readily yield to one
another.(6)"

In the same way adding a gallon of water to a cup of bleach dilutes it and renders it much less potent, 50 state governments maintaining the bulk of political authority spreads authority out and ultimately results in more power in the hands of the people.

Santorum got one thing right. State governments can do some pretty nasty things. And they have. But a look through the annals of history reveals far more horrors perpetrated by centralized, authoritarian government structures. Not only the denial of civil rights, but imprisonment of dissenters, mass murders and genocide. Americans need only look at the actions of their own government during WWII to see the dangers of centralized government power.

On Feb 19, 1942, Pres. Franklin D. Roosevelt signed executive order 9066. The order authorized the Secretary of War and the U.S. Army to create military zones "from which any or all persons may be excluded." The order left who might be excluded to the military's discretion.

This led to the roundup of around 110,000 Japanese-Americans and Japanese citizens living along the west coast of the U.S. and their relocation to internment camps. Between 1,200 and 1,800 people of Japanese descent watched the war from behind barbed wire fences in Hawaii. Of those interned, 62 percent were U.S. citizens.(2) The U.S. government also caged around 11,000 Americans of German ancestry and some 3,000 Italian-Americans.

Mary Tsukamoto was among those rounded up and herded through those gates.

> "We saw all these people behind the fence, looking
> out, hanging onto the wire, and looking out because
> they were anxious to know who was coming in. But I
> will never forget the shocking feeling that human
> beings were behind this fence like animals [crying].
> And we were going to also lose our freedom and walk

inside of that gate and find ourselves...cooped up there...when the gates were shut, we knew that we had lost something that was very precious; that we were no longer free."(8)

If the treatment of the Japanese during World War II doesn't convince you, we really need only to look at the U.S. government's treatment of the Native American populations throughout history. And of course, it took the power of the federal government to maintain the institution of slavery.

But these actions pale compared with the horror wrought by centralized totalitarian regimes around the world, particularly on minority populations. Just after WWI, The Turkish rulers of the Ottoman Empire began the systematic destruction of the Armenian people through mass murder, and mass deportation utilizing forced marches. Between 600,000 and 1.5 million Armenians died. Most historians agree Joseph Stalin orchestrated the Holodomor Famine to neutralize Ukraine as a political factor. Between 2.2 million and 4 million Ukrainians died. And another 3 million or so people died under Stalin's iron-fisted rule over the Soviet Union, some executed, others dying in inhuman conditions in Gulags. Under the rule of Milton Obote and Idi Amin, more than 2 million people were killed, maimed, imprisoned, or forced into exile in Uganda, most of the victims, ethnic minorities. Pol Pot and the Khmer Rouge killed roughly 21 percent of the Cambodian population in the 1970s, some 2 to 5 million souls. Middle Eastern dictatorships and royal rulers regularly deny basic right to their citizens. Women risk jail time for daring to seek an education. Homosexuals face execution, and military and police forces crack down violently when citizens protest the government. And perhaps the most infamous wielder of supreme power: Adolph Hitler. The Nazi regime murdered some 6 million Jews and plunged the world into a war that killed millions more.

Injecting Hitler into any debate generally gets one labeled an extremist, and naysayers tend to brush the point off as mere hyperbole, but it's interesting to note that Der Fuhrer understood the threat "states' rights" posed to his quest to consolidate power and rule Germany as he saw fit. He expressed his disdain for federalism and the roadblocks it placed in front of his plans in Mein Kampf.

*"Since for us the state as such is only a form, but the essential is its content, the nation, the people, it is clear that everything else must be subordinated to its sovereign interests. In particular we **cannot grant to any individual state within the nation and the state representing it state sovereignty and sovereignty in point of political power**"* (Emphasis added)

He went on to write:

"National Socialism as a matter of principle, must lay claim to the right to force its principles on the whole German nation without consideration of previous federated state boundaries, and to educate in its ideas and conceptions. Just as the churches do not feel bound and limited by political boundaries, no more does the National Socialist idea feel limited by the individual state territories of our fatherland. The National Socialist doctrine is not the servant of individual federated states, but shall some day become the master of the German nation. It must determine and reorder the life of a people, and must, therefore, imperiously claim the right to pass over [state] boundaries drawn by a development we have rejected"(9)

Despite the obvious dangers of concentrating power in one large centralized government, most politicians and activists can't resist its allure, despite the fact that centralize governments rank among history's worse killers. After all, politicians and activists want to "get things done." And getting things done proves much easier when you can pass a single act in Washington D.C., applying the force of law across the entire country. Who wants to lobby 50 state legislatures to advance an agenda when you can go to D.C. and do one-stop shopping? As a result, members of both major political parties decry big government and its oppressive reach when it proves convenient, and yet readily embrace and wield federal power when it suits their particular political aims. Conservative Republicans howl in horror at the prospect of the federal government requiring Americans to purchase health insurance and bemoan oppressive EPA regulations, while enthusiastically supporting an unconstitutional "War on Drugs" and nationwide bans on gay marriage. On the other hand, progressives criticize FDA crackdowns on raw milk farmers while supporting countless federal laws and regulation on other activities that don't concern them directly, and fuss about Republican violation of war powers. That is until their guy wants to wage war.

Pragmatism over principle.

Partisans need to wrap their heads around an important fact: when you grant the government power to advance your personal agenda, you also grant the government the power to advance your opponents' agenda. And once you allow government expanded powers, reasoning that you do it for the "common good," how do you stop it when someone decides to use that very power for nefarious purposes? Because when we leave the barn door open for the horses, the pigs will surely follow. Gerald Ford eloquently articulated the danger of granting the government power in order to get our way during a speech to a joint session of Congress in August 1974.

"A government big enough to give you everything you want is a government big enough to take from you everything you have."

In the 1000s and 1100s, William the Conqueror, King Henry I and King Henry II consolidated power in the monarchy in England. Before the death of Henry II, these three kings created and perfected an amazingly efficient system for taxation, dispensing justice and generally administering the Kingdom. The Crown systemized local governance, and even managed to wield power and influence over the Church. This strong centralized monarchal government brought order to a previously chaotic land. But as historian William Sharpe McKechnie points out, "Great as was the power for good of this new instrument in the hands of a wise and justice–loving king, it was equally powerful for evil in the hands of an arrogant, or even of a careless monarch."(10)

In fact the next two English rulers bore this out. King Richard I and King John proved oppressive and tyrannical. Both kings increased taxes at will to fund foreign wars, placing a greater and greater burden on the people. They also tended to make arbitrary judgments. Historian Ralph Turner describes John as possessing "distasteful, even dangerous personality traits", such as pettiness, spitefulness and cruelty.(11) His rule ultimately led to a rebellion of the barons, who forced John to adopt the Magna Carta, limiting the king's power and for the first time, placing government under the rule of law.

The lesson: you should always consider whether you would want your worst enemy to wield the power you grant "your guy."

When faced with the "bigger is badder" argument, supporters of ever expanding federal government will inevitably resort to scare tactics. Without the FDA, grocery stores will sell rotting meat and pharmaceutical companies will flood hospitals with dangerous poisons. Without the department of education, children will graduate from high school unable to read. Do away with the TSA and Americans will face terror in the skies. That is if all of the planes haven't fallen from the heavens without the firm oversight of the FAA. No EPA? Our water will become undrinkable and black smog will fill the sky. Cut the Department of Energy and Americans will be left to read paper books by candlelight. Devolve power from Washington D.C. and millions will starve in the streets, drug abuse will run rampant, the elderly will retire to cardboard boxes and meals of Alpo, and Americans will engage in running gun battles up and down city streets.

In a nutshell, progressives argue that we NEED government to do all of the things it does, Constitution be damned. And we can't trust the state governments to handle things within their own borders; we need the more powerful hand of the feds. Just look at the failure of the states in so many policy areas. Big government apologists will highlight the fact that most state budgets would collapse were it not for the infusion of billions in federal funds, and they gloat over the

latest "conservative" governor crawling with hand out, begging for
FEMA to intervene and assist after the latest flood, fire or hurricane.

But notice the slight-of-hand implicit in the progressive argument.
They support the existence of the system by pointing out the
inevitable manifestation of the system. We have here the ultimate
circular argument. We can't do without the system because the
system does what the system does, so we have to have the system to
do it. It's like a fish living in tidal pool. It can't conceive of life outside
of its three-foot deep, 200-foot wide coral filled haven. From the
fish's point of view, if the tidal pool were to dry up, the entire
universe would cease to exist. It would die a horrible death. Little
does our little fishy realize, he could swim down a narrow channel
and an entire ocean of possibilities would open up before him.

When the feds suck billions of dollars out of the states via taxation,
only breadcrumbs remain for state governments. Of course the states
turn to FEMA in time of disaster. They lack the resources to cope
because the feds syphon so much money off to D.C. And the fact that
FEMA exists excuses the states from truly preparing for a disaster.
They know they can fall back on the federal safety net.

The system itself necessitates and perpetuates the system.

When the federal government promises to provide for our every
need, the average citizen has no incentive to step up and serve her
neighbor. Pull out your state and federal tax returns. Most Americans
don't give that state form a second thought. It represents a pittance
compared to the amount of money confiscated by the IRS. We've
flipped things on their head. The states should collect the majority of
taxes and provide the bulk of government services to its citizens. And
when individual Americans give up close to half of their income in
various taxes and fees, how can they dig deep, reach out and meet
the needs of their neighbors? Washington D.C. has choked the life out
of state governments. It has choked the life out of private
organizations. And it has choked the life out of the average citizen.
The federal government exists as a giant, ubiquitous kudzu plant,

overgrowing everything, strangling the life out of all it covers. A green, mindless unkillable ghost, with tendrils of power spreading from sea to shining sea, wrapping itself around virtually everything. Today, scarcely any part of life in the U.S. remains untouched by the federal government.

And like Kudzu, the feds squeeze out important components of America's political landscape.

State governments stand as the most obvious victims of federal overreach. States can no longer exercise power over those areas, "which, in the ordinary course of affairs, concern the lives, liberties and properties of the people, and the internal order, improvement and prosperity of the State." The federal government took over most state functions years ago. From education to environmental protection, state governments have become virtual spectators as the feds dictate policy and fund initiatives. The fact that the states allowed it to happen, and in many cases encourage it, doesn't make it any less problematic.

And the states don't lie alone wrapped up in a federal vine. Churches and private charities atrophy as the government takes over roles long served by these institutions. Americans now look to Washington D.C. for charity and moral guidance. Jail cells fill and welfare lines grow as church pews empty and private food banks clamor for volunteers. Federal bureaucrats guide Americans' food choices, health choices, and word choices, all the while teaching "correct" modes of thinking. Uncle Sam has replaced our priests, doctors and mothers.

Still, big government advocates continue to promote the federal government as the protector of minorities, completely ignoring the most significant, yet most vulnerable minority – the individual.

A giant painting hangs in the Salvador Dali Museum in St. Petersburg, Fla. titled The Discovery of America by Christopher Columbus.

The canvas measures over 14 feet tall and spans more than nine feet in width. It depicts Columbus landing in America in symbolic fashion. The painting features an intricate hodgepodge of colors, shapes and figures, swirling in a way that almost overwhelms the senses. From a distance, it blends together in almost chaotic fashion. But get up close, and you will notice amazing details, impossible to see from further away. For instance, Dali painted himself into the scene. He depicted himself as a kneeling monk clutching a crucifix. Spears on the right side of the painting hide the image of the crucified Christ. And on the bottom left, you will notice flies, a symbolic nod to a Catalan folk legend about St. Narciso's crypt.

The further one stands away from the painting, the more difficult it becomes to see these amazing details. Individual elements crucial to the story fade away at a distance.

In a similar fashion, political bodies remote from the people they govern lose focus on individuals. Centralized governments respond to groups not people. The significance and relevance of the individual disappears when the government gets too big and too far away from the people.

Proponents of centralized power in the U.S. argue that minorities need a strong federal government to protect them. But politicians and bureaucrats define minorities as groups – blacks, Hispanics, Muslims, gays, etc. They ignore the individual.

In fact, identity politics homogenizes people and sticks them in silos. It strips people of their individual characteristics, their differing opinions and their divergent world views, and pits them against each other based on meaningless criteria such as skin color, or how they have sex or how they worship (or don't). Do we really believe every black person thinks and believes the same things, or that they all behave in like fashion?

David writes in Psalm 139

13 For you created my inmost being;
you knit me together in my mother's womb.
14 I praise you because I am fearfully and wonderfully made;
your works are wonderful,
I know that full well.
15 My frame was not hidden from you

when I was made in the secret place,
when I was woven together in the depths of the earth.
16 Your eyes saw my unformed body;
all the days ordained for me were written in your book
before one of them came to be.

Judeo-Christian thought elevates the individual, teaching that the creator of the universe knows each person individually and deals with us on a personal level.

The point isn't to make a religious statement. It's an example of the universal idea that each of us matters. Each of us counts. Each of us has purpose. Not merely as part of some group, but as unique individuals. We each matter, whether gay or straight, Christian or Muslim, Republican or Democrat, black or white – regardless of our position or station in life. We count because we exist.

Philosopher Emmanuel Kant argued that we should never treat humanity as a means, but as an ends unto itself. In other words, he believed in the dignity of every person, and this fosters the idea of respect for persons.

> *"In the kingdom of ends everything has either a price or a dignity. What has a price can be replaced by something else as its equivalent; what on the other hand is above all price and therefore admits of no equivalent has a dignity.*

> *"What is related to general human inclinations and needs has a market price; that which, even without presupposing a need, conforms with a certain taste, that is, with a delight in the mere purposeless play of our mental powers, has a fancy price; but that which constitutes the condition under which alone something can be an end in itself has not merely a relative worth, that is, a price, but an inner worth, that is, dignity."*(12)

We are each endowed with dignity – in other words each individual possesses a natural, innate right to respect and ethical treatment. We don't come into the world marked with some arbitrary value. Babies don't have $9.99 stamped on their forehead. Each human soul comes into the world with immeasurable worth.

But aloof, centralized government lacks the ability to treat individuals with dignity. In the same way we miss important details when we stand at a distance from Dali's masterpiece, remote government bureaucrats and functionaries cannot see persons. They deal with groups and policies and procedures, ultimately trampling the inalienable rights of the individual like a herd of cattle crushing blades of grass to get to the bale of hay. In advocating for one group, government brushes the dignity of other individuals aside like chaff on the threshing floor.

We lose power over our own lives on a daily basis as nannies in Washington D.C. watch over us with a benevolently tyrannical eye.

Newsflash: the government doesn't have to do all of the stuff it does.

Heck, it doesn't have to do most of the stuff it does.

This goes for state governments as well, but particularly holds true of the federal government, which the framers constituted to serve limited purposes, "principally external objects, as war, peace, negotiation and foreign commerce; with which the last the power of taxation will for the most part be connected."

We have here a complete lack of imagination. Americans have become so conditioned to letting the government do virtually everything; they forget that many other institutions can serve society, and in most cases serve it better than government. I mean, do we really accept the notion that the U.S. Postal Service and the Social Security Administration represent civilization's pinnacle? Do we really believe that if the government got out of the road building business, we'd simply do without roads? Can we not envision industrious, hardworking, Americans filled with ingenuity figuring out some way to travel around the country without federal road programs?

Just because we do things a certain way doesn't mean it's the only way. That's like assuming my route to work each morning constitutes the ONLY route to work. If I stop and looked at a map, I will likely find half a dozen ways to get to the office, and possibly an even better route than the one I take daily out of sheer habit. I certainly wouldn't just stop going to work if I found the route I normally traverse blocked by a sinkhole for a month.

Thomas Woods points out the obvious consequences of rampant federal intervention in his book Rollback.

> "Just as a muscle atrophies from lack of use, civil
> society's ability to manage affairs withers away when
> all of its functions are usurped by an outside force,"
> he wrote. "We have been rendered so helpless and
> dehumanized that we can scarcely imagine how the
> voluntary solutions of civil society might lend
> assistance to people in need without the government
> gun in the ribs."(13)

We have become fish in a tidal pool, incapable of conceiving the political landscape differently. So we accept the status quo and all of the inefficiency, debt and tyranny that goes along with it. We must think differently or we will forever continue getting what we're getting.

When are we going to say, "Enough is enough?"

In 1953, less than two decades after enthusiastically promoting the plant, the government quit advocating the use of Kudzu for erosion control. In 1973, the feds declared it a weed, illustrating the utter ineptitude of the federal government.

But I digress.

The rapid spread of the vine led scientists to begin researching ways to kill Kudzu. Turns out that proved easier said than done. One herbicide actually makes the plant grow faster.

Reining in our overreaching federal government will prove no less problematic. But it's time to start. Americans must begin clearing the landscape of the federal vine, allowing other important institutions to once again bask in the sunlight so that they can thrive and flourish. One-size-fits all solutions handed down from a centralized bureaucracy, completely disconnected from the people, make for crappy policy.

Just look at Kudzu.

The federal government cannot possibly effectively serve as church, charity, police officer, moral leader, doctor, nutritionist, environmental consultant, nanny, etc. etc.

Let the church serve as the church. Let charities administer charity. Let the states tend to matters of the state. And let the individual flourish, making her own mistakes and enjoying her own successes.

Bigger is badder, and the Marshmallow Man continues to grow in both size and appetite. No rational American believes that the United States can simply continue on its current path. We've maxed out the credit card and the bank is calling in the loans. The American people can either take proactive steps to shrink Washington D.C. and gain control of the overreaching federal monster, or the system will eventually collapse on itself.

That's where nullification comes in. The Principles of '98 provide a lethal weapon we can wield to slay the beast. But we have to pick up the sword and use it. The Ghost Busters won't ride in to the rescue.

Ultimately, it's up to us.

We have one last hope.

8

DO WORK!

Most Americans take a lawn care approach to politics.

From around mid-March through October, I spend about 90 minutes every week walking in circles around my yard, ears assailed by a deafening, monotonous drone. When I finish up, the grass looks really nice. Then, about three days later, the lawn begins to take on a bit of a raggedy look. By the next week, I have to repeat the process again.

And again.

And again.

Once I complete my weekly drudgery, I invariably begin pondering ways to make the grass just stop growing. Of course, I can't. Grass grows. That's its nature. Only one way exists to avoid the weekly mowing ritual. Fundamentally change the nature of my yard - as in rip out all of the grass by the roots.

American politics reminds me of lawn care. We take a top down approach. Every four years, political parties, candidates, lobbyists, PACs and everyday citizens spend billions of dollars to choose a president. For more than a year, candidates debate and jockey for position. By the time the general election rolls around, Americans have already endured a seemingly endless primary season. And when it's all said and done, what really changes?

Take the 2008 election pitting John McCain against Barak Obama. Obama won the election promising "hope and change." He painted a McCain victory as an endorsement of "the failed policies of George W. Bush." But really, what actually changed?

With Bush, we had rampant spending, increasing debt and a rapidly growing federal government. President Obama kept right on spending, increased the debt even faster and expanded the scope and power of the federal government. Under Bush, we had war in Iraq and Afghanistan. Under Obama, we had war in Iraq and Afghanistan, with Libya and Yemen thrown in for good measure. Bush signed the Patriot Act into law, including many provisions violating basic due process rights protected by the Constitution. Obama reauthorized it, and signed the 2012 National Defense Authorization Act with indefinite detention provisions included. Under Bush, we got the TSA, running its gloved hands over our bodies and through our stuff. Under Obama, the TSA got scanners, so now they can look at our "stuff." Obama gave us "Obamacare." Bush gave us a prescription drug benefit.

Both presidents oversaw a growing, bloated federal government engaging in unconstitutional acts. Republican or Democrat, it doesn't seem to matter. A Republican administration brought you the Patriot Act, undeclared war, the expansion of entitlements, the Real ID Act, TARP and a continuation of the federal "war on drugs." Thanks to the Democrats, Americans enjoy overreaching EPA mandates, expanding entitlements, auto maker bailouts, undeclared war, government run health care, a continuation of the federal "war on drugs" and FDA raids on Amish farmers. On and on it goes.

After four years witnessing Obama continuing and expanding Bush policies, Republican candidates marched from sea to shining sea promising they would usher in a new era of "limited government" if the voting public would just give them a chance.

Forgive my skepticism.

Tenth Amendment founder and executive director Michael Boldin made a not-so-bold prediction during the primary season preceding the 2012 presidential election.

"No matter who wins in 2012, I guarantee the federal government will be bigger and more intrusive in 2014."

And it's not just the presidency. Americans spend hundreds of millions of dollars on U.S. Senate and Congressional races. In 2008, candidates, political parties and special interests spent $5.3 billion on the presidential, U.S. Senate and U.S. House of Representative races.(1) Top-tier candidates garner nationwide media attention. "Call your Congressman!" or "Call your Senator!" becomes a rallying cry for political activists. And we call. And we email. And we write letters. And we protest. And for the most part, our "representatives" vote however their party power structure dictates.

Oh, they all play a good game. Democrats gain control of Congress and Republicans cry, "The sky is falling." Then two years later, the American public vents its rage, throws the bums out and installs a new set of bums with Rs next to their names. Democrats predict the apocalypse, and two years later we wash, rinse and repeat. In the meantime, the debt grows, the government grows, the bombs keep dropping and the basic structure of the federal government remains unchanged. With few exceptions, and only minor variations, the two major parties follow the same foreign policy and the same domestic policy. Democrats proudly announce their intention to empower the feds. Republicans act in a stealthier manner, talking about cuts and reform, but in reality merely restructuring things to benefit their particular constituencies. Rearranging the deck chairs on the Titanic, as the saying goes.

In the meantime, the Constitution sits under a glass case in the Library of Congress, virtually forgotten.

It seems to me the two parties vying for supremacy in Washington D.C. really represent two sides of the very same coin. They may differ in degree, but not in substance. They may apply power along different avenues, but both parties love to wield the big government stick. And Republicans and Democrats alike show little or no regard for constitutional constraint when it comes to implementing their preferred policy. The conservative will howl in protest at the notion of a federally run health care system, rightfully declaring it outside of the powers delegated to the general government, and then vote to create a Medicare prescription drug benefit. And these same staunch defenders of the Constitution won't bat an eye when the DEA enforces unconstitutional drug laws. In the meantime, Democrats decry unconstitutional, civil liberty violating provisions of the Patriot Act, while pushing for federal gun control laws.

The number of lobbyists roaming the streets of D.C., looking to garner influence in the halls of Congress, attests to the concentration of power in our nation's capital. In 2011, 12,220 registered lobbyists spent $2.45 billion dollars hoping to grease the political rails and gain whatever advantage they believe the government can bestow upon them. (2)

Americans have turned Washington D.C. into the political Mecca. We bow down toward Capitol Hill whenever we want to get something done in the United States, whether affecting economic policy, social policy, public health policy, energy policy, transportation policy, environmental policy, drug policy, agricultural policy, labor policy...the list goes on adnauseum. This does not in any way resemble the Republic envisioned by the Founding Fathers.

Remember Madison's words. Federal powers "few and defined." Powers left to the states and the people, "numerous and indefinite."

So, how do we ever restore the intended balance of power between the state and federal governments? How do we rein in Mr. Stay Puft? Because I don't think a call to Ghostbusters will help us at this point – as cool as a proton pack might be.

First, we must stop assuming Washington D.C. will solve all of America's problems.

Ladies and gentlemen, Washington D.C. **IS** the problem.

Electing a new president, a new senator or a new congressman will never bring about any kind of fundamental change. It's a little like expecting an infant to change her own diaper. Every parent knows that child will sit there in her own filth until the end of time until a big person comes along and changes the soiled, smelly diaper. And a foul stench certainly emanates from the banks of the Potomac.

It's time to change some dirty diapers!

The lawn care approach Americans take to politics focuses on the top, clipping a couple of inches off the grass blades, while leaving the fundamental system underneath unaffected. A look over the last 75 years, or longer, of American politics reveals the failure of this strategy. Albert Einstein gets credit for defining insanity as doing the same thing over and over again, and expecting a different result. By that definition, the time has come to straight jacket the U.S. political establishment. To bring about real change, we must do something to get at the roots. We must work from the bottom up.

As we've seen, the states hold the key.

Nullification provides a powerful tool that can shift authority back to the states and the people where it belongs. If state lawmakers and executives begin standing up to overreaching federal power, saying, "No!" when the folks in D.C. pass acts outside of their authority, only then will we see the federal government begin to respect the intended limits on its power. You can't expect an animal to stay in the proper field without a fence.

It's time to build some fences.

The previous chapters outlined the history of nullification, its philosophical foundation and the importance of decentralizing power. But this book remains nothing more than an academic exercise unless we put the Principles of '98 into action. Until that happens, D.C. will continue to grow and morph into an ever more powerful version of Mr. Stay Puft, rampaging across the fruited plain, devouring everything in its path.

James Madison wrote, "In case of a deliberate, palpable, and dangerous exercise of other powers, not granted by the said compact, the states who are parties thereto, have the right, and are in **duty bound**, to interpose for arresting the progress of the evil, and for maintaining within their respective limits, the authorities, rights and liberties appertaining to them."

Notice Madison didn't call state interposition a nice idea. He didn't hold it up as an option. He didn't say state legislators should step in if they think it politically expedient, or if the pollster says constituents will approve. Madison called it a state's "duty" to take on the federal government on behalf of its citizens. Included in the obligations state legislators and executive officers take on when they swear their oath of office – stand up and protect the life liberty and property of the people they represent. That includes shielding them from overreaching federal power. State officials swear to protect and defend the Constitution of the United States, which includes checking the general government when it seeks to act in a manner contrary to the founding document.

Ultimately, it comes down to you – the United States citizen. You are the final hope!

State senators, representatives, governors and other state officials certainly don't stand at the pinnacle of human morality, wisdom and benevolence. They don't act in ways any more ethical, good intentioned or self-sacrificing than government functionaries in Washington D.C. Like most politicians, they generally act in the manner most politically expedient, not guided by principle. They will follow the lead of lobbyists, special interests and financial donors; unless we make it clear they *must* listen to us if they wish to remain in office.

We the people must hold our state government officials accountable, and push them to do their duty and interpose on our behalf. As we discussed in the chapter on decentralization, Americans potentially wield more access, influence and control over their state governments than they do over the behemoth in D.C. They simply must step up and exercise it. We all have the potential to get in good physical shape. But we have to hit the gym to make it happen. We won't become athletic sitting on the couch eating chips. And we won't ever change our government sitting on our easy chairs watching American Idol.

But the lawn care approach to politics discourages this strategy.

The Kentucky Republican gubernatorial primary in 2011 featured a strong advocate for the Tenth Amendment and a supporter of the principle of nullification on the ballot. But only 10.3 percent of registered voters bothered to turn out to the polls. Out of 2,917,837 registered voters in the Commonwealth, just over 300,000 voted.(3) State officials called it "abysmal." This kind of apathy toward state politics isn't limited to the Bluegrass State. Compared with the time, money and energy focused on national political campaigns, most state level elections scarcely create a blip on the radar screen. Many people can't even name their state representative or senator. And in many state races across the country, candidates simply run unopposed. Officeholders who face no reelection challenge work with little or no accountability – at least not to the people they represent.

Why should they bother with their constituents? They don't need them in order to hold on to and consolidate power.

This must change.

If we ever want to wrest control and power away from Washington D.C. and place the federal government back into its properly prescribed role, the people must take control of their state governments and demand that they serve as a check on federal power, as they were intended to do. That means focusing less attention on who resides in the White House and more attention to who represents us in our state house. As we've seen over the last 100 years, it makes little difference which party controls Capitol Hill or what brand of politician calls 1600 Pennsylvania Avenue home. The federal government balloons regardless.

Power should flow from the people, through the states, to Washington D.C. Not from Washington D.C. down through the states and onto the people. We must work bottom up, starting at the roots. Clipping the top off the grass no longer remains a viable option. This means becoming active in state politics, running for state level offices, and spending time and energy lobbying state representatives. We will win the battle in Nashville, Sacramento and Tallahassee, not Washington D.C.

Along with rousing the public from its general apathy toward state politics, another fundamental shift must occur before the states will possess the power to force change in Washington. State governments must disengage from the carrot and stick game the feds force them to play. D.C. compels states to dance to its tune through federal funding. They dangle the carrot, promising money in exchange for relinquished control over this or that program. Education, health care, transportation, law enforcement, environmental protection – name the policy area and you will likely find federal dollars involved. And with those federal dollars come federal intervention, mandates and criteria. If the states balk at the ever increasing control and heavy handed dictates from Washington, the feds swing the stick, threatening to yank funding for non-compliance. Faced with the loss of millions or even billions of dollars, state officials quickly fall in line.

During health care oral arguments before the Supreme Court in May, 2012, Justice Anthony Kenndey verbalized what we all know.

"It seems to me that they (states) have compromised their status as independent sovereigns because they are so dependent on what the federal government has done."

Ending the carrot and stick routine will prove easier said than done.

In the first quarter of 2009, Uncle Sam became the No. 1 funding source for state governments for the first time in history. States took in more federal money than they did sales tax. More federal money than they did property tax. More federal money than they did state income taxes. The feds doled out $552.1 billion in 2009, according to a U.S. Census Bureau report. The Obama stimulus package accounted for a large part of the jump that year, but the fact remains, states have become more and more dependent on the U.S. Treasury to fill their gaping budget holes. A USA Today story in May 2009 reported that federal funding accounted for about 23 percent of the $2 trillion dollars in state spending. According to the U.S. Census Bureau, our benevolent Uncle outdid himself the following year. The feds handed out some $630.2 billion to the states in 2010. Alaska received the largest amount of money per capita, followed by Wyoming and Delaware. California received the most aid in actual dollars in 2010 - $66.6 billion. (4)

That's a pretty juicy carrot.

And a damn intimidating stick.

The U.S. tax system creates this dependence. Look at your state income tax form and compare it to your IRS forms. For most Americans, state taxes exist as little more than an afterthought on April 15. The federal government sucks enormous sums of money out of the states only to sift it through a vast bureaucracy before handing it back out, putting state governments in a position where they must beg for the money back. How many times have you heard politicians justify earmarks, saying they must play the game to get money taken from their state back into their state?

Today's reality stands 180 degrees opposite of the system envisioned by the founders. States should collect the bulk of taxes, funding the indefinite objects concerning *lives, liberties and properties of the people, and the internal order, improvement and prosperity of the State." Our federal tax bill should remain relatively small.*

If the money won't make the states sing Uncle Sam's tune, he's not above resorting to mob style intimidation. In 2011, the federal government stopped a Texas effort to criminalize invasive TSA searches in its tracks, threatening to turn the Lone Star State into a 'No-Fly Zone.' HB1937 unanimously passed the Texas House on May 13. A week later, the bill passed favorably out of the Senate Transportation and Homeland Security Committee. But a letter delivered to key senators from U.S. Attorney John E. Murphy stopped the bill dead in its tracks.

> *"If HR [sic] 1937 were enacted, the federal government would likely seek an emergency stay of the statute," Murphy wrote. "Unless or until such a stay were granted, TSA would likely be required to cancel any flight or series of flights for which it could not ensure the safety of passengers and crew," he wrote. "We urge that you consider the ramifications of this bill before casting your vote."*

The ominous letter prompted senate sponsor Dan Patrick (R-Houston) to pull the plug on the bill.

He shouldn't have.

At some point, state legislators must summon the courage to face down the federal bullies. Let the feds shut down air travel. Let Congress and the President explain the importance and constitutionality of groping passengers prior to getting on an airplane. I doubt the justification would fly with the majority of Americans. At the time, Dallas served as a hub for one of the world largest air carriers, American Airlines. Continental Airlines operated a hub out of Houston and America's largest discount airline, Southwest, calls Dallas' Love Field home. Imagine the havoc had the feds followed through with their plan. The nation's entire air traffic system would have quickly degenerated into chaos, and the public outcry would most likely have forced the federal government to back down. But the Texas legislators lacked a spine and fell apart under the Department of Justice threat like a paper towel under a water faucet.

It comes back to holding state legislators and executives accountable. The Texas senators knew some Texans would get angry at their failure to pass a bill that garnered a great deal of public support. They anticipated a public outcry and a few rallies outside of the capitol building. But they knew the actual consequences would likely prove minimal. Most of those senators knew they would face little opposition stemming from the TSA fiasco when reelection time rolled around. Heck, by campaign time, the TSA issue will likely be long forgotten.

Now imagine how those men and women would have behaved had they known the Texas public would hold them accountable. If they heard a cacophony of voices demanding they act. If they knew failure would result in consequences – in the form of a pink slip and a trip to the unemployment line. In fact, political pressure did force the issue back in front of the legislature just a few weeks later. Public outcry and a timely video catching Rick Perry obfuscating on the issue compelled the Texas governor to put the TSA bill on the agenda for a special session.(5) The bill ultimately failed to pass in a swirl of political gamesmanship, but the saga reveals how just a little public pressure and activism can impact the political process at the state level. Imagine widespread, determined effort from a large swath of voters applied at the state level. We'd see change, and that change would eventually climb the ladder up to the federal level.

The people hold the keys to power. But for the most part, they fail to put them in the ignition.

The federal government won't change itself. And the state governments won't force the needed changes in D.C. unless we the people demand it. It is imperative that Americans begin applying the same focus, energy and effort at the state level as they have trying to change Washington by electing a new president or congressman.

So what can you do?

Here are a few concrete suggestions to get you involved.

1. **Become active in state politics.** Know who is running for office. Campaign for those who uphold the principles of federalism and oppose those who refuse to stand up for your state's sovereignty.
2. **Educate your state officeholders and candidates.** Give them a copy of this book, along with Tom Wood's book *Nullification: How to Resist Federal Tyranny in the 21st Century.* Make an appointment and go to your state senator and representative's office and talk to them about nullification. You can rest assured; many don't even know about the concept.
3. **Educate the public.** Go to your local activist groups and encourage them to advocate for the *Principles of 98*. Start a blog. Write a letter to the editor. Make a video and post it online. Many Americans don't realize states have the power to force change in D.C., and they will quickly become allies when educated on the principles and history of nullification. Your voice can quickly swell in volume through the power of social media and the Internet. Network with others and leverage the power, speaking in a unified voice.
4. **Lobby your representatives and senators.** Research bills and know when state sovereignty friendly legislation comes before your state's legislature. When it does, demand its passage. Make those phone calls. Send those letters. Make a

trip to your representative's office and explain the importance of the bill. You have a much greater chance at influencing your state legislators than you do changing the vote of your congressional representative or senator. Use that influence where you can wield the most influence. Organize lobbying groups across your state and create an action plan for getting the word out when legislation comes up. Create an email list and send out action alerts when necessary.

5. **Push lawmakers to advance nullification bills.** Find representatives and senators who stand up for your state's sovereignty and encourage them to file nullification and Tenth Amendment related legislation. You will find model legislation on at www.tenthamendmentcenter.com.

6. **Can't find any state legislators willing to stand up for your state's sovereignty? Consider running for office yourself.** Especially if you live in a district where a candidate gets reelected over and over again with no opposition. Even if you fail to get elected, your presence in the campaign will bring Tenth Amendment issues to the forefront and could usher in changes down the road. It will create an opportunity for you to push the agenda into the media spotlight.

7. **Volunteer at the Tenth Amendment Center.** The organization is always looking for volunteers to work at the state level. TAC needs state chapter coordinators to organize these efforts at the state level, along with dedicated soldiers willing to do much-needed legwork. Go to www.tenthamendmentcenter.com and click the "volunteer" link to get more information on how you can get involved.

8. **Support the Tenth Amendment Center financially.** TAC tirelessly works to advance the principles of federalism, constitutional fidelity and nullification. The organization combines education and activism, demanding the government, "Follow the Constitution every issue, every time, no exceptions, no excuses." Even working with a skeleton

staff and a shoe-string budget, the TAC has garnered national attention; its work is quoted in major newspapers, cable news shows and radio programs across the nation. But TAC needs support to keep going and expand its work. Founder and executive director Michael Boldin explains the TAC's needs. "We believe in our work here at the Tenth Amendment Center. We believe that while the path to the Constitution and your liberty might be a long, winding road – the cause is right and just. As more and more people come to believe in these great principles – eventually we'll have a slew of amazing new gifts in this country. Freedom, for example, would be a great new beginning for all of us. Your gift to the Tenth Amendment Center right now will help us continue to play our part in the growth of this great movement...for liberty."

Americans claim they want change. But change will never come about on its own. Change takes work. Metamorphosis requires effort. As long as most Americans remain disengaged from state politics, only rousing themselves from *truTV* or the big ball game long enough to cast a vote in a presidential election every four years, America will continue sliding down a path toward tyranny.

Yes, tyranny – "arbitrary or unrestrained exercise of power; despotic abuse of authority."

Every time Congress passes an unconstitutional act, it abuses its power. Every time a federal agent enforces an unconstitutional act, she abuses her power. Every time the president commits troops to an undeclared war, he abuses his power. It's dangerous and it's immoral. Unrestrained, the federal government will eventually evolve into a tyrannical institution, with no regard for the rights and liberties of the citizens it rules over. One could argue, we're closer to that state than not.

WE must stop it. And to do so, WE must overcome our complacency. WE need some fire in our belly to rouse us from our slumber. British historian Arnold J. Toynbee said, "Apathy can be overcome by enthusiasm, and enthusiasm can only be aroused by two things: first, an ideal, which takes the imagination by storm, and second, a definite intelligible plan for carrying that ideal into practice."

We have ideals - a Constitution conceived by men driven by principles of freedom, liberty and self-government. We have ideals - the Tenth Amendment declaring all powers not delegated to the federal government remain with the states and the people. We have ideals - the Principles of '98 declaring the power of states to just say, "No!" to unwarranted exercise of federal power and the authority to nullify unconstitutional acts.

Now **you** must go out and exercise a definite intelligible plan for carrying these ideals into practice. Do work!

You are our last hope!

And stop asking permission where none is required!

"The liberties of our country, the freedoms of our civil Constitution are worth defending at all hazards; it is our duty to defend them against all attacks. We have received them as a fair inheritance from our worthy ancestors. They purchased them for us with toil and danger and expense of treasure and blood. It will bring a mark of everlasting infamy on the present generation – enlightened as it is – if we should suffer them to be wrested from us by violence without a struggle, or to be cheated out of them by the artifices of designing men."
-Samuel Adams

APPENDIX

Declaration of Independence

When in the Course of human events it becomes necessary for one people to dissolve the political bands which have connected them with another and to assume among the powers of the earth, the separate and equal station to which the Laws of Nature and of Nature's God entitle them, a decent respect to the opinions of mankind requires that they should declare the causes which impel them to the separation.

We hold these truths to be self-evident, that all men are created equal, that they are endowed by their Creator with certain unalienable Rights, that among these are Life, Liberty and the pursuit of Happiness. — That to secure these rights, Governments are instituted among Men, deriving their just powers from the consent of the governed, — That whenever any Form of Government becomes destructive of these ends, it is the Right of the People to alter or to abolish it, and to institute new Government, laying its foundation on such principles and organizing its powers in such form, as to them shall seem most likely to effect their Safety and Happiness. Prudence, indeed, will dictate that Governments long established should not be changed for light and transient causes; and accordingly all experience hath shewn that mankind are more disposed to suffer, while evils are sufferable than to right themselves by abolishing the forms to which they are accustomed. But when a long train of abuses and

usurpations, pursuing invariably the same Object evinces a design to
reduce them under absolute Despotism, it is their right, it is their
duty, to throw off such Government, and to provide new Guards for
their future security. — Such has been the patient sufferance of these
Colonies; and such is now the necessity which constrains them to
alter their former Systems of Government. The history of the present
King of Great Britain is a history of repeated injuries and usurpations,
all having in direct object the establishment of an absolute Tyranny
over these States. To prove this, let Facts be submitted to a candid
world.

He has refused his Assent to Laws, the most wholesome and
necessary for the public good.

He has forbidden his Governors to pass Laws of immediate and
pressing importance, unless suspended in their operation till his
Assent should be obtained; and when so suspended, he has utterly
neglected to attend to them.

He has refused to pass other Laws for the accommodation of large
districts of people, unless those people would relinquish the right of
Representation in the Legislature, a right inestimable to them and
formidable to tyrants only.

He has called together legislative bodies at places unusual,
uncomfortable, and distant from the depository of their Public
Records, for the sole purpose of fatiguing them into compliance with
his measures.

He has dissolved Representative Houses repeatedly, for opposing
with manly firmness his invasions on the rights of the people.

He has refused for a long time, after such dissolutions, to cause
others to be elected, whereby the Legislative Powers, incapable of
Annihilation, have returned to the People at large for their exercise;
the State remaining in the mean time exposed to all the dangers of
invasion from without, and convulsions within.

He has endeavoured to prevent the population of these States; for
that purpose obstructing the Laws for Naturalization of Foreigners;

refusing to pass others to encourage their migrations hither, and raising the conditions of new Appropriations of Lands.

He has obstructed the Administration of Justice by refusing his Assent to Laws for establishing Judiciary Powers.

He has made Judges dependent on his Will alone for the tenure of their offices, and the amount and payment of their salaries.

He has erected a multitude of New Offices, and sent hither swarms of Officers to harass our people and eat out their substance.

He has kept among us, in times of peace, Standing Armies without the Consent of our legislatures.

He has affected to render the Military independent of and superior to the Civil Power.

He has combined with others to subject us to a jurisdiction foreign to our constitution, and unacknowledged by our laws; giving his Assent to their Acts of pretended Legislation:

For quartering large bodies of armed troops among us:

For protecting them, by a mock Trial from punishment for any Murders which they should commit on the Inhabitants of these States:

For cutting off our Trade with all parts of the world:

For imposing Taxes on us without our Consent:

For depriving us in many cases, of the benefit of Trial by Jury:

For transporting us beyond Seas to be tried for pretended offences:

For abolishing the free System of English Laws in a neighbouring Province, establishing therein an Arbitrary government, and enlarging its Boundaries so as to render it at once an example and fit instrument for introducing the same absolute rule into these Colonies

For taking away our Charters, abolishing our most valuable Laws and altering fundamentally the Forms of our Governments:

For suspending our own Legislatures, and declaring themselves invested with power to legislate for us in all cases whatsoever.

He has abdicated Government here, by declaring us out of his Protection and waging War against us.

He has plundered our seas, ravaged our coasts, burnt our towns, and destroyed the lives of our people.

He is at this time transporting large Armies of foreign Mercenaries to compleat the works of death, desolation, and tyranny, already begun with circumstances of Cruelty & Perfidy scarcely paralleled in the most barbarous ages, and totally unworthy the Head of a civilized nation.

He has constrained our fellow Citizens taken Captive on the high Seas to bear Arms against their Country, to become the executioners of their friends and Brethren, or to fall themselves by their Hands.

He has excited domestic insurrections amongst us, and has endeavoured to bring on the inhabitants of our frontiers, the merciless Indian Savages whose known rule of warfare, is an undistinguished destruction of all ages, sexes and conditions.

In every stage of these Oppressions We have Petitioned for Redress in the most humble terms: Our repeated Petitions have been answered only by repeated injury. A Prince, whose character is thus marked by every act which may define a Tyrant, is unfit to be the ruler of a free people.

Nor have We been wanting in attentions to our British brethren. We have warned them from time to time of attempts by their legislature to extend an unwarrantable jurisdiction over us. We have reminded them of the circumstances of our emigration and settlement here. We have appealed to their native justice and magnanimity, and we have conjured them by the ties of our common kindred to disavow these usurpations, which would inevitably interrupt our connections and correspondence. They too have been deaf to the voice of justice and of consanguinity. We must, therefore, acquiesce in the necessity, which denounces our Separation, and hold them, as we hold the rest of mankind, Enemies in War, in Peace Friends.

We, therefore, the Representatives of the united States of America, in General Congress, Assembled, appealing to the Supreme Judge of the world for the rectitude of our intentions, do, in the Name, and by Authority of the good People of these Colonies, solemnly publish and declare, That these united Colonies are, and of Right ought to be Free and Independent States, that they are Absolved from all Allegiance to the British Crown, and that all political connection between them and the State of Great Britain, is and ought to be totally dissolved; and that as Free and Independent States, they have full Power to levy War, conclude Peace, contract Alliances, establish Commerce, and to do all other Acts and Things which Independent States may of right do. — And for the support of this Declaration, with a firm reliance on the protection of Divine Providence, we mutually pledge to each other our Lives, our Fortunes, and our sacred Honor.

The Constitution of the United States

Preamble

We the People of the United States, in Order to form a more perfect Union, establish Justice, insure domestic Tranquility, provide for the common defence, promote the general Welfare, and secure the Blessings of Liberty to ourselves and our Posterity, do ordain and establish this Constitution for the United States of America.

Article I - The Legislative Branch

Section 1 - The Legislature

All legislative Powers herein granted shall be vested in a Congress of the United States, which shall consist of a Senate and House of Representatives.

Section 2 - The House

The House of Representatives shall be composed of Members chosen every second Year by the People of the several States, and the Electors in each State shall have the Qualifications requisite for Electors of the most numerous Branch of the State Legislature.

No Person shall be a Representative who shall not have attained to the Age of twenty five Years, and been seven Years a Citizen of the United States, and who shall not, when elected, be an Inhabitant of that State in which he shall be chosen.

(Representatives and direct Taxes shall be apportioned among the several States which may be included within this Union, according to their respective Numbers, which shall be determined by adding to the whole Number of free Persons, including those bound to Service for a Term of Years, and excluding Indians not taxed, three fifths of all other Persons.) (The previous sentence in parentheses was modified by the 14th Amendment, section 2.) The actual Enumeration shall be made within three Years after the first Meeting of the Congress of the United States, and within every subsequent Term of ten Years, in such Manner as they shall by Law direct. The Number of Representatives shall not exceed one for every thirty Thousand, but each State shall have at Least one Representative; and until such enumeration shall be made, the State of New Hampshire shall be entitled to chuse three, Massachusetts eight, Rhode Island and Providence Plantations one, Connecticut five, New York six, New Jersey four, Pennsylvania eight, Delaware one, Maryland six, Virginia ten, North Carolina five, South Carolina five and Georgia three.

When vacancies happen in the Representation from any State, the Executive Authority thereof shall issue Writs of Election to fill such Vacancies.

The House of Representatives shall chuse their Speaker and other Officers; and shall have the sole Power of Impeachment.

Section 3 - The Senate

The Senate of the United States shall be composed of two Senators from each State, (chosen by the Legislature thereof,) (The preceding words in parentheses superseded by 17th Amendment, section 1.) for six Years; and each Senator shall have one Vote.

Immediately after they shall be assembled in Consequence of the first Election, they shall be divided as equally as may be into three Classes. The Seats of the Senators of the first Class shall be vacated at the Expiration of the second Year, of the second Class at the Expiration of the fourth Year, and of the third Class at the Expiration of the sixth Year, so that one third may be chosen every second Year; (and if Vacancies happen by Resignation, or otherwise, during the Recess of the Legislature of any State, the Executive thereof may make temporary Appointments until the next Meeting of the Legislature, which shall then fill such Vacancies.) (The preceding words in parentheses were superseded by the 17th Amendment, section 2.)

No person shall be a Senator who shall not have attained to the Age of thirty Years, and been nine Years a Citizen of the United States, and who shall not, when elected, be an Inhabitant of that State for which he shall be chosen.

The Vice President of the United States shall be President of the Senate, but shall have no Vote, unless they be equally divided.

The Senate shall chuse their other Officers, and also a President pro tempore, in the absence of the Vice President, or when he shall exercise the Office of President of the United States.

The Senate shall have the sole Power to try all Impeachments. When sitting for that Purpose, they shall be on Oath or Affirmation. When the President of the United States is tried, the Chief Justice shall preside: And no Person shall be convicted without the Concurrence of two thirds of the Members present.

Judgment in Cases of Impeachment shall not extend further than to removal from Office, and disqualification to hold and enjoy any Office of honor, Trust or Profit under the United States: but the Party convicted shall nevertheless be liable and subject to Indictment, Trial, Judgment and Punishment, according to Law.

Section 4 - Elections, Meetings

The Times, Places and Manner of holding Elections for Senators and Representatives, shall be prescribed in each State by the Legislature thereof; but the Congress may at any time by Law make or alter such Regulations, except as to the Place of Chusing Senators.

The Congress shall assemble at least once in every Year, and such Meeting shall (be on the first Monday in December,) (The preceding words in parentheses were superseded by the 20th Amendment, section 2.) unless they shall by Law appoint a different Day.

Section 5 - Membership, Rules, Journals, Adjournment

Each House shall be the Judge of the Elections, Returns and Qualifications of its own Members, and a Majority of each shall constitute a Quorum to do Business; but a smaller number may adjourn from day to day, and may be authorized to compel the

Attendance of absent Members, in such Manner, and under such Penalties as each House may provide.

Each House may determine the Rules of its Proceedings, punish its Members for disorderly Behavior, and, with the Concurrence of two-thirds, expel a Member.

Each House shall keep a Journal of its Proceedings, and from time to time publish the same, excepting such Parts as may in their Judgment require Secrecy; and the Yeas and Nays of the Members of either House on any question shall, at the Desire of one fifth of those Present, be entered on the Journal.

Neither House, during the Session of Congress, shall, without the Consent of the other, adjourn for more than three days, nor to any other Place than that in which the two Houses shall be sitting.

Section 6 - Compensation

(The Senators and Representatives shall receive a Compensation for their Services, to be ascertained by Law, and paid out of the Treasury of the United States.) (The preceding words in parentheses were modified by the 27th Amendment.) They shall in all Cases, except Treason, Felony and Breach of the Peace, be privileged from Arrest during their Attendance at the Session of their respective Houses, and in going to and returning from the same; and for any Speech or Debate in either House, they shall not be questioned in any other Place.

No Senator or Representative shall, during the Time for which he was elected, be appointed to any civil Office under the Authority of the United States which shall have been created, or the Emoluments whereof shall have been increased during such time; and no Person holding any Office under the United States, shall be a Member of either House during his Continuance in Office.

Section 7 - Revenue Bills, Legislative Process, Presidential Veto

All bills for raising Revenue shall originate in the House of Representatives; but the Senate may propose or concur with Amendments as on other Bills.

Every Bill which shall have passed the House of Representatives and the Senate, shall, before it become a Law, be presented to the President of the United States; If he approve he shall sign it, but if not he shall return it, with his Objections to that House in which it shall have originated, who shall enter the Objections at large on their Journal, and proceed to reconsider it. If after such Reconsideration two thirds of that House shall agree to pass the Bill, it shall be sent, together with the Objections, to the other House, by which it shall likewise be reconsidered, and if approved by two thirds of that House, it shall become a Law. But in all such Cases the Votes of both Houses shall be determined by Yeas and Nays, and the Names of the Persons voting for and against the Bill shall be entered on the Journal of each House respectively. If any Bill shall not be returned by the President within ten Days (Sundays excepted) after it shall have been presented to him, the Same shall be a Law, in like Manner as if he had signed it, unless the Congress by their Adjournment prevent its Return, in which Case it shall not be a Law.

Every Order, Resolution, or Vote to which the Concurrence of the Senate and House of Representatives may be necessary (except on a question of Adjournment) shall be presented to the President of the United States; and before the Same shall take Effect, shall be approved by him, or being disapproved by him, shall be repassed by two thirds of the Senate and House of Representatives, according to the Rules and Limitations prescribed in the Case of a Bill.

Section 8 - Powers of Congress

The Congress shall have Power To lay and collect Taxes, Duties, Imposts and Excises, to pay the Debts and provide for the common Defence and general Welfare of the United States; but all Duties, Imposts and Excises shall be uniform throughout the United States;

To borrow money on the credit of the United States;

To regulate Commerce with foreign Nations, and among the several States, and with the Indian Tribes;

To establish an uniform Rule of Naturalization, and uniform Laws on the subject of Bankruptcies throughout the United States;

To coin Money, regulate the Value thereof, and of foreign Coin, and fix the Standard of Weights and Measures;

To provide for the Punishment of counterfeiting the Securities and current Coin of the United States;

To establish Post Offices and Post Roads;

To promote the Progress of Science and useful Arts, by securing for limited Times to Authors and Inventors the exclusive Right to their respective Writings and Discoveries;

To constitute Tribunals inferior to the supreme Court;

To define and punish Piracies and Felonies committed on the high Seas, and Offenses against the Law of Nations;

To declare War, grant Letters of Marque and Reprisal, and make Rules concerning Captures on Land and Water;

To raise and support Armies, but no Appropriation of Money to that Use shall be for a longer Term than two Years;

To provide and maintain a Navy;

To make Rules for the Government and Regulation of the land and naval Forces;

To provide for calling forth the Militia to execute the Laws of the Union, suppress Insurrections and repel Invasions;

To provide for organizing, arming, and disciplining, the Militia, and for governing such Part of them as may be employed in the Service of the United States, reserving to the States respectively, the Appointment of the Officers, and the Authority of training the Militia according to the discipline prescribed by Congress;

To exercise exclusive Legislation in all Cases whatsoever, over such District (not exceeding ten Miles square) as may, by Cession of particular States, and the acceptance of Congress, become the Seat of the Government of the United States, and to exercise like Authority over all Places purchased by the Consent of the Legislature of the State in which the Same shall be, for the Erection of Forts, Magazines, Arsenals, dock-Yards, and other needful Buildings; And

To make all Laws which shall be necessary and proper for carrying into Execution the foregoing Powers, and all other Powers vested by this Constitution in the Government of the United States, or in any Department or Officer thereof.

Section 9 - Limits on Congress

The Migration or Importation of such Persons as any of the States now existing shall think proper to admit, shall not be prohibited by the Congress prior to the Year one thousand eight hundred and eight, but a tax or duty may be imposed on such Importation, not exceeding ten dollars for each Person.

The privilege of the Writ of Habeas Corpus shall not be suspended, unless when in Cases of Rebellion or Invasion the public Safety may require it.

No Bill of Attainder or ex post facto Law shall be passed.

(No capitation, or other direct, Tax shall be laid, unless in Proportion to the Census or Enumeration herein before directed to be taken.) (Section in parentheses clarified by the 16th Amendment.)

No Tax or Duty shall be laid on Articles exported from any State.

No Preference shall be given by any Regulation of Commerce or Revenue to the Ports of one State over those of another: nor shall Vessels bound to, or from, one State, be obliged to enter, clear, or pay Duties in another.

No Money shall be drawn from the Treasury, but in Consequence of Appropriations made by Law; and a regular Statement and Account of the Receipts and Expenditures of all public Money shall be published from time to time.

No Title of Nobility shall be granted by the United States: And no Person holding any Office of Profit or Trust under them, shall, without the Consent of the Congress, accept of any present, Emolument, Office, or Title, of any kind whatever, from any King, Prince or foreign State.

Section 10 - Powers prohibited of States

No State shall enter into any Treaty, Alliance, or Confederation; grant Letters of Marque and Reprisal; coin Money; emit Bills of Credit; make any Thing but gold and silver Coin a Tender in Payment of Debts; pass any Bill of Attainder, ex post facto Law, or Law impairing the Obligation of Contracts, or grant any Title of Nobility.

No State shall, without the Consent of the Congress, lay any Imposts or Duties on Imports or Exports, except what may be absolutely necessary for executing it's inspection Laws: and the net Produce of all Duties and Imposts, laid by any State on Imports or Exports, shall be for the Use of the Treasury of the United States; and all such Laws shall be subject to the Revision and Controul of the Congress.

No State shall, without the Consent of Congress, lay any duty of Tonnage, keep Troops, or Ships of War in time of Peace, enter into any Agreement or Compact with another State, or with a foreign Power, or engage in War, unless actually invaded, or in such imminent Danger as will not admit of delay.

Article II - The Executive Branch

Section 1 - The President
The executive Power shall be vested in a President of the United States of America. He shall hold his Office during the Term of four Years, and, together with the Vice-President chosen for the same Term, be elected, as follows:

Each State shall appoint, in such Manner as the Legislature thereof may direct, a Number of Electors, equal to the whole Number of Senators and Representatives to which the State may be entitled in the Congress: but no Senator or Representative, or Person holding an Office of Trust or Profit under the United States, shall be appointed an Elector.

(The Electors shall meet in their respective States, and vote by Ballot for two persons, of whom one at least shall not lie an Inhabitant of the same State with themselves. And they shall make a List of all the Persons voted for, and of the Number of Votes for each; which List they shall sign and certify, and transmit sealed to the Seat of the Government of the United States, directed to the President of the Senate. The President of the Senate shall, in the Presence of the Senate and House of Representatives, open all the Certificates, and the Votes shall then be counted. The Person having the greatest Number of Votes shall be the President, if such Number be a Majority of the whole Number of Electors appointed; and if there be more than one who have such Majority, and have an equal Number of Votes, then the House of Representatives shall immediately chuse by Ballot one of them for President; and if no Person have a Majority, then from the five highest on the List the said House shall in like Manner chuse the President. But in chusing the President, the Votes shall be taken by States, the Representation from each State having one Vote; a quorum for this Purpose shall consist of a Member or Members from two-thirds of the States, and a Majority of all the States shall be necessary to a Choice. In every Case, after the Choice of the President, the Person having the greatest Number of Votes of the Electors shall be the Vice President. But if there should remain two or more who have equal Votes, the Senate shall chuse from them by Ballot the Vice-President.) (This clause in parentheses was superseded by the 12th Amendment.)

The Congress may determine the Time of chusing the Electors, and the Day on which they shall give their Votes; which Day shall be the same throughout the United States.

No person except a natural born Citizen, or a Citizen of the United States, at the time of the Adoption of this Constitution, shall be eligible to the Office of President; neither shall any Person be eligible to that Office who shall not have attained to the Age of thirty-five Years, and been fourteen Years a Resident within the United States.

(In Case of the Removal of the President from Office, or of his Death, Resignation, or Inability to discharge the Powers and Duties of the said Office, the same shall devolve on the Vice President, and the Congress may by Law provide for the Case of Removal, Death, Resignation or Inability, both of the President and Vice President, declaring what Officer shall then act as President, and such Officer shall act accordingly, until the Disability be removed, or a President shall be elected.) (This clause in parentheses has been modified by the 20th and 25th Amendments.)

The President shall, at stated Times, receive for his Services, a Compensation, which shall neither be increased nor diminished during the Period for which he shall have been elected, and he shall not receive within that Period any other Emolument from the United States, or any of them.

Before he enter on the Execution of his Office, he shall take the following Oath or Affirmation:

"I do solemnly swear (or affirm) that I will faithfully execute the Office of President of the United States, and will to the best of my Ability, preserve, protect and defend the Constitution of the United States."

Section 2 - Civilian Power over Military, Cabinet, Pardon Power, Appointments

The President shall be Commander in Chief of the Army and Navy of the United States, and of the Militia of the several States, when called into the actual Service of the United States; he may require the Opinion, in writing, of the principal Officer in each of the executive Departments, upon any subject relating to the Duties of their respective Offices, and he shall have Power to Grant Reprieves and Pardons for Offenses against the United States, except in Cases of Impeachment.

He shall have Power, by and with the Advice and Consent of the Senate, to make Treaties, provided two thirds of the Senators present concur; and he shall nominate, and by and with the Advice and Consent of the Senate, shall appoint Ambassadors, other public Ministers and Consuls, Judges of the supreme Court, and all other Officers of the United States, whose Appointments are not herein otherwise provided for, and which shall be established by Law: but the Congress may by Law vest the Appointment of such inferior Officers, as they think proper, in the President alone, in the Courts of Law, or in the Heads of Departments.

The President shall have Power to fill up all Vacancies that may happen during the Recess of the Senate, by granting Commissions which shall expire at the End of their next Session.

Section 3 - State of the Union, Convening Congress

He shall from time to time give to the Congress Information of the State of the Union, and recommend to their Consideration such Measures as he shall judge necessary and expedient; he may, on extraordinary Occasions, convene both Houses, or either of them, and in Case of Disagreement between them, with Respect to the Time of Adjournment, he may adjourn them to such Time as he shall think proper; he shall receive Ambassadors and other public Ministers; he shall take Care that the Laws be faithfully executed, and shall Commission all the Officers of the United States.

Section 4 - Disqualification

The President, Vice President and all civil Officers of the United States, shall be removed from Office on Impeachment for, and Conviction of, Treason, Bribery, or other high Crimes and Misdemeanors.

Article III - The Judicial Branch

Section 1 - Judicial powers

The judicial Power of the United States, shall be vested in one supreme Court, and in such inferior Courts as the Congress may from time to time ordain and establish. The Judges, both of the supreme and inferior Courts, shall hold their Offices during good Behavior, and shall, at stated Times, receive for their Services a Compensation which shall not be diminished during their Continuance in Office.

Section 2 - Trial by Jury, Original Jurisdiction, Jury Trials

(The judicial Power shall extend to all Cases, in Law and Equity, arising under this Constitution, the Laws of the United States, and Treaties made, or which shall be made, under their Authority; to all Cases affecting Ambassadors, other public Ministers and Consuls; to all Cases of admiralty and maritime Jurisdiction; to Controversies to which the United States shall be a Party; to Controversies between two or more States; between a State and Citizens of another State; between Citizens of different States; between Citizens of the same State claiming Lands under Grants of different States, and between a State, or the Citizens thereof, and foreign States, Citizens or Subjects.) (This section in parentheses is modified by the 11th Amendment.)

In all Cases affecting Ambassadors, other public Ministers and Consuls, and those in which a State shall be Party, the supreme Court shall have original Jurisdiction. In all the other Cases before mentioned, the supreme Court shall have appellate Jurisdiction, both as to Law and Fact, with such Exceptions, and under such Regulations as the Congress shall make.

The Trial of all Crimes, except in Cases of Impeachment, shall be by Jury; and such Trial shall be held in the State where the said Crimes shall have been committed; but when not committed within any State, the Trial shall be at such Place or Places as the Congress may by Law have directed.

Section 3 - Treason

Treason against the United States, shall consist only in levying War against them, or in adhering to their Enemies, giving them Aid and Comfort. No Person shall be convicted of Treason unless on the Testimony of two Witnesses to the same overt Act, or on Confession in open Court.

The Congress shall have power to declare the Punishment of Treason, but no Attainder of Treason shall work Corruption of Blood, or Forfeiture except during the Life of the Person attainted.
Article IV - The States

Section 1 - Each State to Honor all others

Full Faith and Credit shall be given in each State to the public Acts, Records, and judicial Proceedings of every other State. And the Congress may by general Laws prescribe the Manner in which such Acts, Records and Proceedings shall be proved, and the Effect thereof.

Section 2 - State citizens, Extradition

The Citizens of each State shall be entitled to all Privileges and Immunities of Citizens in the several States.

A Person charged in any State with Treason, Felony, or other Crime, who shall flee from Justice, and be found in another State, shall on demand of the executive Authority of the State from which he fled, be delivered up, to be removed to the State having Jurisdiction of the Crime.

(No Person held to Service or Labour in one State, under the Laws thereof, escaping into another, shall, in Consequence of any Law or Regulation therein, be discharged from such Service or Labour, But shall be delivered up on Claim of the Party to whom such Service or Labour may be due.) (This clause in parentheses is superseded by the 13th Amendment.)

Section 3 - New States

New States may be admitted by the Congress into this Union; but no new States shall be formed or erected within the Jurisdiction of any other State; nor any State be formed by the Junction of two or more States, or parts of States, without the Consent of the Legislatures of the States concerned as well as of the Congress.

The Congress shall have Power to dispose of and make all needful Rules and Regulations respecting the Territory or other Property belonging to the United States; and nothing in this Constitution shall be so construed as to Prejudice any Claims of the United States, or of any particular State.

Section 4 - Republican government

The United States shall guarantee to every State in this Union a Republican Form of Government, and shall protect each of them against Invasion; and on Application of the Legislature, or of the Executive (when the Legislature cannot be convened) against domestic Violence.
Article V - Amendment

The Congress, whenever two thirds of both Houses shall deem it necessary, shall propose Amendments to this Constitution, or, on the Application of the Legislatures of two thirds of the several States, shall call a Convention for proposing Amendments, which, in either Case, shall be valid to all Intents and Purposes, as part of this Constitution, when ratified by the Legislatures of three fourths of the several States, or by Conventions in three fourths thereof, as the one or the other Mode of Ratification may be proposed by the Congress; Provided that no Amendment which may be made prior to the Year One thousand eight hundred and eight shall in any Manner affect the first and fourth Clauses in the Ninth Section of the first Article; and that no State, without its Consent, shall be deprived of its equal Suffrage in the Senate.

Article VI - Debts, Supremacy, Oaths

All Debts contracted and Engagements entered into, before the Adoption of this Constitution, shall be as valid against the United States under this Constitution, as under the Confederation.

This Constitution, and the Laws of the United States which shall be made in Pursuance thereof; and all Treaties made, or which shall be made, under the Authority of the United States, shall be the supreme Law of the Land; and the Judges in every State shall be bound thereby, any Thing in the Constitution or Laws of any State to the Contrary notwithstanding.

The Senators and Representatives before mentioned, and the Members of the several State Legislatures, and all executive and judicial Officers, both of the United States and of the several States, shall be bound by Oath or Affirmation, to support this Constitution; but no religious Test shall ever be required as a Qualification to any Office or public Trust under the United States.
Article VII - Ratification Documents

The Ratification of the Conventions of nine States, shall be sufficient for the Establishment of this Constitution between the States so ratifying the Same.

Done in Convention by the Unanimous Consent of the States present the Seventeenth Day of September in the Year of our Lord one thousand seven hundred and Eighty seven and of the Independence of the United States of America the Twelfth. In Witness whereof We have hereunto subscribed our Names.

Bill of Rights

THE Conventions of a number of the States having at the time of their adopting the Constitution, expressed a desire, in order to prevent misconstruction or abuse of its powers, that further declaratory and restrictive clauses should be added: And as extending the ground of public confidence in the Government, will best insure the beneficent ends of its institution

RESOLVED by the Senate and House of Representatives of the United States of America, in Congress assembled, two thirds of both Houses concurring, that the following Articles be proposed to the Legislatures of the several States, as Amendments to the Constitution of the United States, all or any of which Articles, when ratified by three fourths of the said Legislatures, to be valid to all intents and purposes, as part of the said Constitution; viz.:

ARTICLES in addition to, and Amendment of the Constitution of the United States of America, proposed by Congress, and ratified by the

Legislatures of the several States, pursuant to the fifth Article of the original Constitution.

Amendment 1 - Freedom of Religion, Press, Expression. Ratified 12/15/1791.

Congress shall make no law respecting an establishment of religion, or prohibiting the free exercise thereof; or abridging the freedom of speech, or of the press; or the right of the people peaceably to assemble, and to petition the Government for a redress of grievances.

Amendment 2 - Right to Bear Arms. Ratified 12/15/1791.

A well regulated Militia, being necessary to the security of a free State, the right of the people to keep and bear Arms, shall not be infringed.

Amendment 3 - Quartering of Soldiers. Ratified 12/15/1791.

No Soldier shall, in time of peace be quartered in any house, without the consent of the Owner, nor in time of war, but in a manner to be prescribed by law.

Amendment 4 - Search and Seizure. Ratified 12/15/1791.

The right of the people to be secure in their persons, houses, papers, and effects, against unreasonable searches and seizures, shall not be violated, and no Warrants shall issue, but upon probable cause, supported by Oath or affirmation, and particularly describing the place to be searched, and the persons or things to be seized.

Amendment 5 - Trial and Punishment, Compensation for Takings. Ratified 12/15/1791.

No person shall be held to answer for a capital, or otherwise infamous crime, unless on a presentment or indictment of a Grand Jury, except in cases arising in the land or naval forces, or in the Militia, when in actual service in time of War or public danger; nor shall any person be subject for the same offense to be twice put in jeopardy of life or limb; nor shall be compelled in any criminal case to be a witness against himself, nor be deprived of life, liberty, or property, without due process of law; nor shall private property be taken for public use, without just compensation.

Amendment 6 - Right to Speedy Trial, Confrontation of Witnesses. Ratified 12/15/1791.

In all criminal prosecutions, the accused shall enjoy the right to a speedy and public trial, by an impartial jury of the State and district wherein the crime shall have been committed, which district shall have been previously ascertained by law, and to be informed of the nature and cause of the accusation; to be confronted with the witnesses against him; to have compulsory process for obtaining witnesses in his favor, and to have the Assistance of Counsel for his defence.

Amendment 7 - Trial by Jury in Civil Cases. Ratified 12/15/1791.

In Suits at common law, where the value in controversy shall exceed twenty dollars, the right of trial by jury shall be preserved, and no fact tried by a jury, shall be otherwise re-examined in any Court of the United States, than according to the rules of the common law.

Amendment 8 - Cruel and Unusual Punishment. Ratified 12/15/1791.

Excessive bail shall not be required, nor excessive fines imposed, nor cruel and unusual punishments inflicted.

Amendment 9 - Construction of Constitution. Ratified 12/15/1791.

The enumeration in the Constitution, of certain rights, shall not be construed to deny or disparage others retained by the people.

Amendment 10 - Powers of the States and People. Ratified 12/15/1791.

The powers not delegated to the United States by the Constitution, nor prohibited by it to the States, are reserved to the States respectively, or to the people.

Amendment 11 - Judicial Limits. Ratified 2/7/1795.

The Judicial power of the United States shall not be construed to extend to any suit in law or equity, commenced or prosecuted against one of the United States by Citizens of another State, or by Citizens or Subjects of any Foreign State.

Amendment 12 - Choosing the President, Vice-President. Ratified 6/15/1804.

The Electors shall meet in their respective states, and vote by ballot for President and Vice-President, one of whom, at least, shall not be an inhabitant of the same state with themselves; they shall name in their ballots the person voted for as President, and in distinct ballots the person voted for as Vice-President, and they shall make distinct lists of all persons voted for as President, and of all persons voted for as Vice-President and of the number of votes for each, which lists they shall sign and certify, and transmit sealed to the seat of the government of the United States, directed to the President of the Senate;

The President of the Senate shall, in the presence of the Senate and House of Representatives, open all the certificates and the votes shall then be counted;

The person having the greatest Number of votes for President, shall be the President, if such number be a majority of the whole number of Electors appointed; and if no person have such majority, then from the persons having the highest numbers not exceeding three on the list of those voted for as President, the House of Representatives shall choose immediately, by ballot, the President. But in choosing the President, the votes shall be taken by states, the representation from each state having one vote; a quorum for this purpose shall consist of a member or members from two-thirds of the states, and a majority of all the states shall be necessary to a choice. And if the House of Representatives shall not choose a President whenever the right of choice shall devolve upon them, before the fourth day of March next following, then the Vice-President shall act as President, as in the case of the death or other constitutional disability of the President.

The person having the greatest number of votes as Vice-President, shall be the Vice-President, if such number be a majority of the whole number of Electors appointed, and if no person have a majority, then from the two highest numbers on the list, the Senate shall choose the Vice-President; a quorum for the purpose shall consist of two-thirds of the whole number of Senators, and a majority of the whole number shall be necessary to a choice. But no person constitutionally ineligible to the office of President shall be eligible to that of Vice-President of the United States.

Amendment 13 - Slavery Abolished. Ratified 12/6/1865.

1. Neither slavery nor involuntary servitude, except as a punishment for crime whereof the party shall have been duly convicted, shall exist within the United States, or any place subject to their jurisdiction.

2. Congress shall have power to enforce this article by appropriate legislation.

Amendment 14 - Citizenship Rights. Ratified 7/9/1868.

1. All persons born or naturalized in the United States, and subject to the jurisdiction thereof, are citizens of the United States and of the State wherein they reside. No State shall make or enforce any law which shall abridge the privileges or immunities of citizens of the United States; nor shall any State deprive any person of life, liberty, or property, without due process of law; nor deny to any person within its jurisdiction the equal protection of the laws.

2. Representatives shall be apportioned among the several States according to their respective numbers, counting the whole number of persons in each State, excluding Indians not taxed. But when the right to vote at any election for the choice of electors for President and Vice-President of the United States, Representatives in Congress, the Executive and Judicial officers of a State, or the members of the Legislature thereof, is denied to any of the male inhabitants of such State, being twenty-one years of age, and citizens of the United States, or in any way abridged, except for participation in rebellion, or other crime, the basis of representation therein shall be reduced in the proportion which the number of such male citizens shall bear to

the whole number of male citizens twenty-one years of age in such State.

3. No person shall be a Senator or Representative in Congress, or elector of President and Vice-President, or hold any office, civil or military, under the United States, or under any State, who, having previously taken an oath, as a member of Congress, or as an officer of the United States, or as a member of any State legislature, or as an executive or judicial officer of any State, to support the Constitution of the United States, shall have engaged in insurrection or rebellion against the same, or given aid or comfort to the enemies thereof. But Congress may by a vote of two-thirds of each House, remove such disability.

4. The validity of the public debt of the United States, authorized by law, including debts incurred for payment of pensions and bounties for services in suppressing insurrection or rebellion, shall not be questioned. But neither the United States nor any State shall assume or pay any debt or obligation incurred in aid of insurrection or rebellion against the United States, or any claim for the loss or emancipation of any slave; but all such debts, obligations and claims shall be held illegal and void.

5. The Congress shall have power to enforce, by appropriate legislation, the provisions of this article.

Amendment 15 - Race No Bar to Vote. Ratified 2/3/1870.

1. The right of citizens of the United States to vote shall not be denied or abridged by the United States or by any State on account of race, color, or previous condition of servitude.

2. The Congress shall have power to enforce this article by appropriate legislation.

Amendment 16 - Status of Income Tax Clarified. Ratified 2/3/1913.

The Congress shall have power to lay and collect taxes on incomes, from whatever source derived, without apportionment among the several States, and without regard to any census or enumeration.

Amendment 17 - Senators Elected by Popular Vote. Ratified 4/8/1913.

The Senate of the United States shall be composed of two Senators from each State, elected by the people thereof, for six years; and each Senator shall have one vote. The electors in each State shall have the qualifications requisite for electors of the most numerous branch of the State legislatures.

When vacancies happen in the representation of any State in the Senate, the executive authority of such State shall issue writs of election to fill such vacancies: Provided, That the legislature of any State may empower the executive thereof to make temporary appointments until the people fill the vacancies by election as the legislature may direct.

This amendment shall not be so construed as to affect the election or term of any Senator chosen before it becomes valid as part of the Constitution.

Amendment 18 - Liquor Abolished. Ratified 1/16/1919. Repealed by Amendment 21, 12/5/1933.

1. After one year from the ratification of this article the manufacture, sale, or transportation of intoxicating liquors within, the importation thereof into, or the exportation thereof from the United States and all territory subject to the jurisdiction thereof for beverage purposes is hereby prohibited.

2. The Congress and the several States shall have concurrent power to enforce this article by appropriate legislation.

3. This article shall be inoperative unless it shall have been ratified as an amendment to the Constitution by the legislatures of the several States, as provided in the Constitution, within seven years from the date of the submission hereof to the States by the Congress.

Amendment 19 - Women's Suffrage. Ratified 8/18/1920.

The right of citizens of the United States to vote shall not be denied or abridged by the United States or by any State on account of sex.

Congress shall have power to enforce this article by appropriate legislation.

Amendment 20 - Presidential, Congressional Terms. Ratified 1/23/1933.

1. The terms of the President and Vice President shall end at noon on the 20th day of January, and the terms of Senators and Representatives at noon on the 3d day of January, of the years in which such terms would have ended if this article had not been ratified; and the terms of their successors shall then begin.

2. The Congress shall assemble at least once in every year, and such meeting shall begin at noon on the 3d day of January, unless they shall by law appoint a different day.

3. If, at the time fixed for the beginning of the term of the President, the President elect shall have died, the Vice President elect shall become President. If a President shall not have been chosen before the time fixed for the beginning of his term, or if the President elect shall have failed to qualify, then the Vice President elect shall act as President until a President shall have qualified; and the Congress may by law provide for the case wherein neither a President elect nor a Vice President elect shall have qualified, declaring who shall then act as President, or the manner in which one who is to act shall be selected, and such person shall act accordingly until a President or Vice President shall have qualified.

4. The Congress may by law provide for the case of the death of any of the persons from whom the House of Representatives may choose a President whenever the right of choice shall have devolved upon them, and for the case of the death of any of the persons from whom the Senate may choose a Vice President whenever the right of choice shall have devolved upon them.

5. Sections 1 and 2 shall take effect on the 15th day of October following the ratification of this article.

6. This article shall be inoperative unless it shall have been ratified as an amendment to the Constitution by the legislatures of three-fourths of the several States within seven years from the date of its submission.

Amendment 21 - Amendment 18 Repealed. Ratified 12/5/1933.

1. The eighteenth article of amendment to the Constitution of the United States is hereby repealed.

2. The transportation or importation into any State, Territory, or possession of the United States for delivery or use therein of intoxicating liquors, in violation of the laws thereof, is hereby prohibited.

3. The article shall be inoperative unless it shall have been ratified as an amendment to the Constitution by conventions in the several States, as provided in the Constitution, within seven years from the date of the submission hereof to the States by the Congress.

Amendment 22 - Presidential Term Limits. Ratified 2/27/1951.

1. No person shall be elected to the office of the President more than twice, and no person who has held the office of President, or acted as President, for more than two years of a term to which some other person was elected President shall be elected to the office of the President more than once. But this Article shall not apply to any person holding the office of President, when this Article was proposed by the Congress, and shall not prevent any person who may be holding the office of President, or acting as President, during the term within which this Article becomes operative from holding the office of President or acting as President during the remainder of such term.

2. This article shall be inoperative unless it shall have been ratified as an amendment to the Constitution by the legislatures of three-fourths of the several States within seven years from the date of its submission to the States by the Congress.

Amendment 23 - Presidential Vote for District of Columbia. Ratified 3/29/1961.

1. The District constituting the seat of Government of the United States shall appoint in such manner as the Congress may direct: A number of electors of President and Vice President equal to the whole number of Senators and Representatives in Congress to which the District would be entitled if it were a State, but in no event more than the least populous State; they shall be in addition to those appointed by the States, but they shall be considered, for the purposes of the election of President and Vice President, to be electors appointed by a State; and they shall meet in the District and perform such duties as provided by the twelfth article of amendment.

2. The Congress shall have power to enforce this article by appropriate legislation.

Amendment 24 - Poll Tax Barred. Ratified 1/23/1964.

1. The right of citizens of the United States to vote in any primary or other election for President or Vice President, for electors for President or Vice President, or for Senator or Representative in Congress, shall not be denied or abridged by the United States or any State by reason of failure to pay any poll tax or other tax.

2. The Congress shall have power to enforce this article by appropriate legislation.

Amendment 25 - Presidential Disability and Succession. Ratified 2/10/1967.

1. In case of the removal of the President from office or of his death or resignation, the Vice President shall become President.

2. Whenever there is a vacancy in the office of the Vice President, the President shall nominate a Vice President who shall take office upon confirmation by a majority vote of both Houses of Congress.

3. Whenever the President transmits to the President pro tempore of the Senate and the Speaker of the House of Representatives his

written declaration that he is unable to discharge the powers and duties of his office, and until he transmits to them a written declaration to the contrary, such powers and duties shall be discharged by the Vice President as Acting President.

4. Whenever the Vice President and a majority of either the principal officers of the executive departments or of such other body as Congress may by law provide, transmit to the President pro tempore of the Senate and the Speaker of the House of Representatives their written declaration that the President is unable to discharge the powers and duties of his office, the Vice President shall immediately assume the powers and duties of the office as Acting President.

Thereafter, when the President transmits to the President pro tempore of the Senate and the Speaker of the House of Representatives his written declaration that no inability exists, he shall resume the powers and duties of his office unless the Vice President and a majority of either the principal officers of the executive department or of such other body as Congress may by law provide, transmit within four days to the President pro tempore of the Senate and the Speaker of the House of Representatives their written declaration that the President is unable to discharge the powers and duties of his office. Thereupon Congress shall decide the issue, assembling within forty eight hours for that purpose if not in session. If the Congress, within twenty one days after receipt of the latter written declaration, or, if Congress is not in session, within twenty one days after Congress is required to assemble, determines by two thirds vote of both Houses that the President is unable to discharge the powers and duties of his office, the Vice President shall continue to discharge the same as Acting President; otherwise, the President shall resume the powers and duties of his office.

Amendment 26 - Voting Age Set to 18 Years. Ratified 7/1/1971.

1. The right of citizens of the United States, who are eighteen years of age or older, to vote shall not be denied or abridged by the United States or by any State on account of age.

2. The Congress shall have power to enforce this article by appropriate legislation.

Amendment 27 - Limiting Changes to Congressional Pay. Ratified 5/7/1992.

No law, varying the compensation for the services of the Senators and Representatives, shall take effect, until an election of Representatives shall have intervened.

Kentucky Resolutions of 1798
Jefferson's draft

1. *Resolved,* That the several States composing, the United States of America, are not united on the principle of unlimited submission to their general government; but that, by a compact under the style and title of a Constitution for the United States, and of amendments thereto, they constituted a general government for special purposes — delegated to that government certain definite powers, reserving, each State to itself, the residuary mass of right to their own self-government; and that whensoever the general government assumes undelegated powers, its acts are unauthoritative, void, and of no force: that to this compact each State acceded as a State, and is an integral part, its co-States forming, as to itself, the other party: that the government created by this compact was not made the exclusive or final judge of the extent of the powers delegated to itself; since that would have made its discretion, and not the Constitution, the measure of its powers; but that, as in all other cases of compact among powers having no common judge, each party has an equal right to judge for itself, as well of infractions as of the mode and measure of redress.

2. *Resolved,* That the Constitution of the United States, having delegated to Congress a power to punish treason, counterfeiting the securities and current coin of the United States, piracies, and felonies committed on the high seas, and offenses against the law of nations, and no other crimes, whatsoever; and it being true as a general principle, and one of the amendments to the Constitution having also declared, that "the powers not delegated to the United States by the Constitution, not prohibited by it to the States, are reserved to the States respectively, or to the people," therefore the act of Congress, passed on the 14th day of July, 1798, and intituled "An Act in addition to the act intituled An Act for the punishment of certain crimes against the United States," as also the act passed by them on the — day of June, 1798, intituled "An Act to punish frauds committed on the bank of the United States," (and all their other acts which assume to create, define, or punish crimes, other than those so enumerated in the Constitution,) are altogether void, and of no force; and that the power to create, define, and punish such other crimes is reserved,

and, of right, appertains solely and exclusively to the respective States, each within its own territory.

3. *Resolved*, That it is true as a general principle, and is also expressly declared by one of the amendments to the Constitutions, that "the powers not delegated to the United States by the Constitution, our prohibited by it to the States, are reserved to the States respectively, or to the people"; and that no power over the freedom of religion, freedom of speech, or freedom of the press being delegated to the United States by the Constitution, nor prohibited by it to the States, all lawful powers respecting the same did of right remain, and were reserved to the States or the people: that thus was manifested their determination to retain to themselves the right of judging how far the licentiousness of speech and of the press may be abridged without lessening their useful freedom, and how far those abuses which cannot be separated from their use should be tolerated, rather than the use be destroyed. And thus also they guarded against all abridgment by the United States of the freedom of religious opinions and exercises, and retained to themselves the right of protecting the same, as this State, by a law passed on the general demand of its citizens, had already protected them from all human restraint or interference. And that in addition to this general principle and express declaration, another and more special provision has been made by one of the amendments to the Constitution, which expressly declares, that "Congress shall make no law respecting an establishment of religion, or prohibiting the free exercise thereof, or abridging the freedom of speech or of the press": thereby guarding in the same sentence, and under the same words, the freedom of religion, of speech, and of the press: insomuch, that whatever violated either, throws down the sanctuary which covers the others, arid that libels, falsehood, and defamation, equally with heresy and false religion, are withheld from the cognizance of federal tribunals. That, therefore, the act of Congress of the United States, passed on the 14th day of July, 1798, intituled "An Act in addition to the act intituled An Act for the punishment of certain crimes against the United States," which does abridge the freedom of the press, is not law, but is altogether void, and of no force.

4. *Resolved*, That alien friends are under the jurisdiction and protection of the laws of the State wherein they are: that no power

over them has been delegated to the United States, nor prohibited to the individual States, distinct from their power over citizens. And it being true as a general principle, and one of the amendments to the Constitution having also declared, that "the powers not delegated to the United States by the Constitution, nor prohibited by it to the States, are reserved to the States respectively, or to the people," the act of the Congress of the United States, passed on the — day of July, 1798, intituled "An Act concerning aliens," which assumes powers over alien friends, not delegated by the Constitution, is not law, but is altogether void, and of no force.

5. *Resolved.* That in addition to the general principle, as well as the express declaration, that powers not delegated are reserved, another and more special provision, inserted in the Constitution from abundant caution, has declared that "the migration or importation of such persons as any of the States now existing shall think proper to admit, shall not be prohibited by the Congress prior to the year 1808" that this commonwealth does admit the migration of alien friends, described as the subject of the said act concerning aliens: that a provision against prohibiting their migration, is a provision against all acts equivalent thereto, or it would be nugatory: that to remove them when migrated, is equivalent to a prohibition of their migration, and is, therefore, contrary to the said provision of the Constitution, and void.

6. *Resolved,* That the imprisonment of a person under the protection of the laws of this commonwealth, on his failure to obey the simple order of the President to depart out of the United States, as is undertaken by said act intituled "An Act concerning aliens" is contrary to the Constitution, one amendment to which has provided that "no person shalt be deprived of liberty without due progress of law"; and that another having provided that "in all criminal prosecutions the accused shall enjoy the right to public trial by an impartial jury, to be informed of the nature and cause of the accusation, to be confronted with the witnesses against him, to have compulsory process for obtaining witnesses in his favor, and to have the assistance of counsel for his defense;" the same act, undertaking to authorize the President to remove a person out of the United States, who is under the protection of the law, on his own suspicion, without accusation, without jury, without public trial, without confrontation of the

witnesses against him, without heating witnesses in his favor, without defense, without counsel, is contrary to the provision also of the Constitution, is therefore not law, but utterly void, and of no force: that transferring the power of judging any person, who is under the protection of the laws from the courts, to the President of the United States, as is undertaken by the same act concerning aliens, is against the article of the Constitution which provides that "the judicial power of the United States shall be vested in courts, the judges of which shall hold their offices during good behavior"; and that the said act is void for that reason also. And it is further to be noted, that this transfer of judiciary power is to that magistrate of the general government who already possesses all the Executive, and a negative on all Legislative powers.

7. *Resolved*, That the construction applied by the General Government (as is evidenced by sundry of their proceedings) to those parts of the Constitution of the United States which delegate to Congress a power "to lay and collect taxes, duties, imports, and excises, to pay the debts, and provide for the common defense and general welfare of the United States," and "to make all laws which shall be necessary and proper for carrying into execution, the powers vested by the Constitution in the government of the United States, or in any department or officer thereof," goes to the destruction of all limits prescribed to their powers by the Constitution: that words meant by the instrument to be subsidiary only to the execution of limited powers, ought not to be so construed as themselves to give unlimited powers, nor a part to be so taken as to destroy the whole residue of that instrument: that the proceedings of the General Government under color of these articles, will be a fit and necessary subject of revisal and correction, at a time of greater tranquillity, while those specified in the preceding resolutions call for immediate redress.

8th. *Resolved*, That a committee of conference and correspondence be appointed, who shall have in charge to communicate the preceding resolutions to the Legislatures of the several States: to assure them that this commonwealth continues in the same esteem of their friendship and union which it has manifested from that moment at which a common danger first suggested a common union: that it considers union, for specified national purposes, and particularly to those specified in their late federal compact, to be friendly, to the peace, happiness and prosperity of all the States: that faithful to that compact, according to the plain intent and meaning in which it was understood and acceded to by the several parties, it is sincerely anxious for its preservation: that it does also believe, that to take from the States all the powers of self-government and transfer them to a general and consolidated government, without regard to the special delegations and reservations solemnly agreed to in that compact, is not for the peace, happiness or prosperity of these States; and that therefore this commonwealth is determined, as it doubts not its co-States are, to submit to undelegated, and consequently unlimited powers in no man, or body of men on earth: that in cases of an abuse of the delegated powers, the members of the general government, being chosen by the people, a change by the people would be the constitutional remedy; but, where powers are assumed which have not been delegated, a nullification of the act is the rightful remedy: that every State has a natural right in cases not within the compact, (*casus non fœderis*) to nullify of their own authority all assumptions of power by others within their limits: that without this right, they would be under the dominion, absolute and unlimited, of whosoever might exercise this right of judgment for them: that nevertheless, this commonwealth, from motives of regard and respect for its co States, has wished to communicate with them on the subject: that with them alone it is proper to communicate, they alone being parties to the compact, and solely authorized to judge in the last resort of the powers exercised under it, Congress being not a party, but merely the creature of the compact, and subject as to its assumptions of power to the final judgment of those by whom, and for whose use itself and its powers were all created and modified: that if the acts before specified should stand, these conclusions would flow from them; that the general government may place any act they think proper on the list of crimes and punish it themselves whether enumerated or not enumerated by the constitution as cognizable by them: that they may transfer its cognizance to the President, or any other person, who may himself be the accuser, counsel, judge and jury, whose suspicions may be the evidence, his order the sentence, his officer the executioner, and his breast the sole record of the transaction: that a very numerous and valuable description of the inhabitants of these States being, by this precedent, reduced, as outlaws, to the absolute dominion of one man, and the barrier of the Constitution thus swept away from us all, no ramparts now remains against the passions and the powers of a majority in Congress to protect from a like exportation, or other more grievous punishment, the minority of the same body, the legislatures, judges, governors and counsellors of the States, nor their other peaceable inhabitants, who may venture to reclaim the constitutional rights and liberties of the States and people, or who for other causes, good or bad, may be obnoxious to the views, or marked by the suspicions of the President, or be thought dangerous to his or their election, or other interests, public or personal; that the friendless alien has indeed been selected as the safest subject of a first experiment; but the citizen will soon follow, or rather, has already followed, for already has a sedition act marked him as its prey: that these and successive acts of the same character, unless arrested at the threshold, necessarily drive these States into revolution and blood and will furnish new calumnies against republican government, and new pretexts for those who wish it to be believed that man cannot be governed but by a rod of iron: that it would be a dangerous delusion were a confidence in the men of our choice to silence our fears for the safety of our rights: that confidence is everywhere the parent of despotism — free government is founded in jealousy, and not in confidence; it is jealousy and not confidence which prescribes limited constitutions, to bind down those whom we are obliged to trust with power: that our Constitution has accordingly fixed the limits to which, and no further, our confidence may go; and let the honest advocate of confidence read the Alien and Sedition acts, and say if the Constitution has not been wise in fixing limits to the government it created, and whether we should be wise in destroying those limits, Let him say what the government is, if it be not a tyranny, which the men of our choice have con erred on our President, and the President of our choice has assented to, and accepted over the friendly stranger to whom the mild spirit of our country and its law have pledged hospitality and protection: that the men of our choice have more respected the bare suspicion of the President, than the solid right of innocence, the claims of justification, the sacred force of truth, and the forms and substance of law and justice. In questions of powers, then, let no more be heard of confidence in man, but bind him down from mischief by the chains of the Constitution. That this commonwealth does therefore call on its co-States for an expression of their sentiments on the acts concerning aliens and for the punishment of certain crimes herein before specified, plainly declaring whether these acts are or are not authorized by the federal compact. And it doubts not that their sense will be so announced as to prove their attachment unaltered to limited government, weather general or particular. And that the rights and liberties of their co-States will be exposed to no dangers by remaining embarked in a common bottom with their own. That they will concur with this commonwealth in considering the said acts as so palpably against the Constitution as to amount to an undisguised declaration that that compact is not meant to be the measure of the powers of the General Government, but that it will proceed in the exercise over these States, of all powers whatsoever: that they will view this as seizing the rights of the States, and consolidating them in the hands of the General Government, with a power assumed to bind the States (not merely as the cases made federal, casus fœderis but), in all cases whatsoever, by laws made, not with their consent, but by others against their consent: that this would be to surrender the form of government we have chosen, and live under one deriving its powers from its own will, and not from our authority; and that the co-States, recurring to their natural right in cases not made federal, will concur in declaring these acts void, and of no force, and will each take measures of its own for providing that neither these acts, nor any others of the General Government not plainly and intentionally authorized by the Constitution, shalt be exercised within their respective territories.

9th. *Resolved*, That the said committee be authorized to communicate by writing or personal conference, at any times or places whatever, with any person or persons who may be appointed by any one or more co-States to correspond or confer with them; and that they lay their proceedings before the next session of Assembly.

Kentucky Resolutions of 1799
As passed by Kentucky General Assembly

THE representatives of the good people of this commonwealth in general assembly convened, having maturely considered the answers of sundry states in the Union, to their resolutions passed at the last session, respecting certain unconstitutional laws of Congress, commonly called the alien and sedition laws, would be faithless indeed to themselves, and to those they represent, were they silently to acquiesce in principles and doctrines attempted to be maintained in all those answers, that of Virginia only excepted. To again enter the field of argument, and attempt more fully or forcibly to expose the unconstitutionality of those obnoxious laws, would, it is apprehended be as unnecessary as unavailing.

We cannot however but lament, that in the discussion of those interesting subjects, by sundry of the legislatures of our sister states, unfounded suggestions, and uncandid insinuations, derogatory of the true character and principles of the good people of this commonwealth, have been substituted in place of fair reasoning and sound argument. Our opinions of those alarming measures of the general government, together with our reasons for those opinions, were detailed with decency and with temper, and submitted to the discussion and judgment of our fellow citizens throughout the Union. Whether the decency and temper have been observed in the answers of most of those states who have denied or attempted to obviate the great truths contained in those resolutions, we have now only to submit to a candid world. Faithful to the true principles of the federal union, unconscious of any designs to disturb the harmony of that Union, and anxious only to escape the fangs of despotism, the good people of this commonwealth are regardless of censure or calumniation.

Least however the silence of this commonwealth should be construed into an acquiescence in the doctrines and principles advanced and attempted to be maintained by the said answers, or least those of our fellow citizens throughout the Union, who so widely differ from us on those important subjects, should be deluded by the expectation, that we shall be deterred from what we conceive our duty; or shrink from the principles contained in those resolutions: therefore.

RESOLVED, That this commonwealth considers the federal union, upon the terms and for the purposes specified in the late compact, as conducive to the liberty and happiness of the several states: That it does now unequivocally declare its attachment to the Union, and to that compact, agreeable to its obvious and real intention, and will be among the last to seek its dissolution: That if those who administer the general government be permitted to transgress the limits fixed by that compact, by a total disregard to the special delegations of power therein contained, annihilation of the state governments, and the erection upon their ruins, of a general consolidated government, will be the inevitable consequence: That the principle and construction contended for by sundry of the state legislatures, that the general government is the exclusive judge of the extent of the powers delegated to it, stop nothing short of despotism; since the discretion of those who administer the government, and not the constitution, would be the measure of their powers: That the several states who formed that instrument, being sovereign and independent, have the unquestionable right to judge of its infraction; and that a nullification, by those sovereignties, of all unauthorized acts done under colour of that instrument, is the rightful remedy: That this commonwealth does upon the most deliberate reconsideration declare, that the said alien and sedition laws, are in their opinion, palpable violations of the said constitution; and however cheerfully it may be disposed to surrender its opinion to a majority of its sister states in matters of ordinary or doubtful policy; yet, in momentous regulations like the present, which so vitally wound the best rights of the citizen, it would consider a silent acquiescence as highly criminal: That although this commonwealth as a party to the federal compact; will bow to the laws of the Union, yet it does at the same time declare, that it will not now, nor ever hereafter, cease to oppose in a constitutional manner, every attempt from what quarter soever offered, to violate that compact:

AND FINALLY, in order that no pretexts or arguments may be drawn from a supposed acquiescence on the part of this commonwealth in the constitutionality of those laws, and be thereby used as precedents for similar future violations of federal compact; this commonwealth does now enter against them, its SOLEMN PROTEST.

Approved December 3rd, 1799.

Virginia Resolutions of 1798

Authored by James Madison, As Passed by Virginia General Assembly

RESOLVED, That the General Assembly of Virginia, doth unequivocally express a firm resolution to maintain and defend the Constitution of the United States, and the Constitution of this State, against every aggression either foreign or domestic, and that they will support the government of the United States in all measures warranted by the former.

That this assembly most solemnly declares a warm attachment to the Union of the States, to maintain which it pledges all its powers; and that for this end, it is their duty to watch over and oppose every infraction of those principles which constitute the only basis of that Union, because a faithful observance of them, can alone secure it's existence and the public happiness.

That this Assembly doth explicitly and peremptorily declare, that it views the powers of the federal government, as resulting from the compact, to which the states are parties; as limited by the plain sense and intention of the instrument constituting the compact; as no further valid that they are authorized by the grants enumerated in that compact; and that in case of a deliberate, palpable, and dangerous exercise of other powers, not granted by the said compact, the states who are parties thereto, have the right, and are in duty bound, to interpose for arresting the progress of the evil, and for maintaining within their respective limits, the authorities, rights and liberties appertaining to them.

That the General Assembly doth also express its deep regret, that a spirit has in sundry instances, been manifested by the federal government, to enlarge its powers by forced constructions of the constitutional charter which defines them; and that implications have appeared of a design to expound certain general phrases (which having been copied from the very limited grant of power, in the former articles of confederation were the less liable to be misconstrued) so as to destroy the meaning and effect, of the particular enumeration which necessarily explains and limits the general phrases; and so as to consolidate the states by degrees, into one sovereignty, the obvious tendency and inevitable consequence of which would be, to transform the present republican system of the United States, into an absolute, or at best a mixed monarchy.

That the General Assembly doth particularly protest against the palpable and alarming infractions of the Constitution, in the two late cases of the "Alien and Sedition Acts" passed at the last session of Congress; the first of which exercises a power no where delegated to the federal government, and which by uniting legislative and judicial powers to those of executive, subverts the general principles of free government; as well as the particular organization, and positive provisions of the federal constitution; and the other of which acts, exercises in like manner, a power not delegated by the constitution, but on the contrary, expressly and positively forbidden by one of the amendments thereto; a power, which more than any other, ought to produce universal alarm, because it is levelled against that right of freely examining public characters and measures, and of free communication among the people thereon, which has ever been justly deemed, the only effectual guardian of every other right.

That this state having by its Convention, which ratified the federal Constitution, expressly declared, that among other essential rights, "the Liberty of Conscience and of the Press cannot be cancelled, abridged, restrained, or modified by any authority of the United States," and from its extreme anxiety to guard these rights from every possible attack of sophistry or ambition, having with other states, recommended an amendment for that purpose, which amendment was, in due time, annexed to the Constitution; it would mark a reproachable inconsistency, and criminal degeneracy, if an indifference were now shewn, to the most palpable violation of one of the Rights, thus declared and secured; and to the establishment of a precedent which may be fatal to the other.

That the good people of this commonwealth, having ever felt, and continuing to feel, the most sincere affection for their brethren of the other states; the truest anxiety for establishing and perpetuating the union of all; and the most scrupulous fidelity to that constitution, which is the pledge of mutual friendship, and the instrument of mutual happiness; the General Assembly doth solemnly appeal to the like dispositions of the other states, in confidence that they will concur with this commonwealth in declaring, as it does hereby declare, that the acts aforesaid, are unconstitutional; and that the necessary and proper measures will be taken by each, for co-operating with this state, in maintaining the Authorities, Rights, and Liberties, referred to the States respectively, or to the people.

That the Governor be desired, to transmit a copy of the foregoing Resolutions to the executive authority of each of the other states, with a request that the same may be communicated to the Legislature thereof; and that a copy be furnished to each of the Senators and Representatives representing this state in the Congress of the United States.

Agreed to by the Senate, December 24, 1798.

Ratification of the Constitution by the State of Virginia, June 26, 1788

WE the Delegates of the people of Virginia, duly elected in pursuance of a recommendation from the General Assembly, and now met in Convention, having fully and freely investigated and discussed the proceedings of the Federal Convention, and being prepared as well as the most mature deliberation hath enabled us, to decide thereon, **DO** in the name and in behalf of the people of Virginia, declare and make known that the powers granted under the Constitution, being derived from the people of the United States may be resumed by them whensoever the same shall be perverted to their injury or oppression, and that every power not granted thereby remains with them and at their will: that therefore no right of any denomination, can be cancelled, abridged, restrained or modified, by the Congress, by the Senate or House of Representatives acting in any capacity, by the President or any department or officer of the United States, except in those instances in which power is given by the Constitution for those purposes: and that among other essential rights, the liberty of conscience and of the press cannot be cancelled, abridged, restrained or modified by any authority of the United States.

With these impressions, with a solemn appeal to the searcher of hearts for the purity of our intentions, and under the conviction, that, whatsoever imperfections may exist in the Constitution, ought rather to be examined in the mode prescribed therein, than to bring the Union into danger by a delay, with a hope of obtaining amendments previous to the ratification:

We the said Delegates, in the name and in behalf of the people of Virginia, do by these presents assent to, and ratify the Constitution recommended on the seventeenth day of September, one thousand seven hundred and eighty seven, by the Foederal Convention for the Government of the United States; hereby announcing to all those whom it may concern, that the said Constitution is binding upon the said People, according to an authentic copy hereto annexed, in the words following:

On motion, Ordered, That the Secretary of this Convention cause to be engrossed, forthwith, two fair copies of the form of ratification, and of the proposed Constitution of Government, as recommended by the Foederal Convention on the seventeenth day of September, one thousand seven hundred and eighty seven.

MR. Wythe reported, from the Committee appointed, such amendments to the proposed Constitution of Government for the United States, as were by them deemed necessary to be recommended to the consideration of the Congress which shall first assemble under the said Constitution, to be acted upon according to the mode prescribed in the fifth article thereof; and he read the same in his place, and afterwards delivered them in at the clerk's table, where the same were again read, and are as followeth:

That there be a Declaration or Bill of Rights asserting and securing from encroachment the essential and unalienable rights of the people in some such manner as the following:

1st. That there are certain natural rights of which men when they form a social compact cannot deprive or divest their posterity, among which are the enjoyment of life, and liberty, with the means of acquiring, possessing and protecting property, and pursuing and obtaining happiness and safety.

2d. That all power is naturally vested in, and consequently derived from, the people; that magistrates therefore are their trustees, and agents, and at all times amenable to them.

3d. That the Government ought to be instituted for the common benefit, protection and security of the people; and that the doctrine of non-resistance against arbitrary power and oppression, is absurd, slavish, and destructive to the good and happiness of mankind.

4th. That no man or set of men are entitled to exclusive or separate public emoluments or privileges from the community, but in consideration of public services; which not being descendible, neither ought the offices of magistrate, legislator or judge, or any other public office to be hereditary.

5th. That the legislative, executive and judiciary powers of government should be separate and distinct, and that the members of the two first may be restrained from oppression by feeling and participating the public burthens, they should at fixed periods be reduced to a private station, return into the mass of the people; and the vacancies be supplied by certain and regular elections, in which all or any part of the former members to be eligible or ineligible, as the rules of the Constitution of Government, and the laws shall direct.

6th. That elections of Representatives in the legislature ought to be free and frequent, and all men having sufficient evidence of permanent common interest with, and attachment to the community, ought to have the right of suffrage: and no aid, charge, tax or fee can be set, rated, or levied upon the people without their own consent, or that of their representatives, so elected, nor can they be bound by any law, to which they have not in like manner assented for the public good.

7th. That all power of suspending laws, or the execution of laws by any authority without the consent of the representatives, of the people in the legislature, is injurious to their rights, and ought not to be exercised.

8th. That in all capital and criminal prosecutions, a man hath a right to demand the cause and nature of his accusation, to be confronted with the accusers and witnesses, to call for evidence and be allowed counsel in his favor, and to a fair and speedy trial by an impartial jury of his vicinage, without whose unanimous consent he cannot be found guilty (except in the government of the land and naval forces) nor can he be compelled to give evidence against himself.

9th. That no freeman ought to be taken, imprisoned, or disseized of his freehold, liberties, privileges or franchises, or outlawed or exiled, or in any manner destroyed or deprived of his life, liberty, or property but by the law of the land.

10th. That every freeman restrained of his liberty is entitled to a remedy to enquire into the lawfulness thereof, and to remove the same, if unlawful, and that such remedy ought not to be denied nor delayed.

11th. That in controversies respecting property, and in suits between man and man, the ancient trial by jury is one of the greatest securities to the rights of the people, and ought to remain sacred and inviolable.

12th. That every freeman ought to find a certain remedy by recourse to the laws for all injuries and wrongs he may receive in his person, property, or character. He ought to obtain right and justice freely without sale, completely and without denial, promptly and without delay, and that all establishments, or regulations contravening these rights, are oppressive and unjust.

13th. That excessive bail ought not to be required, nor excessive fines imposed, nor cruel and unusual punishments inflicted.

14th. That every freeman has a right to be secure from all unreasonable searches, and seizures of his person, his papers, and property; all warrants therefore to search suspected places, or seize any freeman, his papers or property, without information upon oath (or affirmation of a person religiously scrupulous of taking an oath) of legal and sufficient cause, are grievous and oppressive, and all general warrants to search suspected places, or to apprehend any suspected person without specially naming or describing the place or person, are dangerous and ought not to be granted.

15th. That the people have a right peaceably to assemble together to consult for the common good, or to instruct their representatives; and that every freeman has a right to petition or apply to the Legislature for redress of grievances.

16th. That the people have a right to freedom of speech, and of writing and publishing their sentiments; that the freedom of the press is one of the greatest bulwarks of liberty, and ought not to be violated.

17th. That the people have a right to keep and bear arms; that a well regulated militia composed of the body of the people trained to arms, is the proper, natural and safe defence of a free state. That standing armies in time of peace are dangerous to liberty, and therefore ought to be avoided, as far as the circumstances and protection of the community will admit; and that in all cases, the military should be under strict subordination to and governed by the civil power.

18th. That no soldier in time of peace ought to be quartered in any house without the consent of the owner, and in time of war in such manner only as the laws direct.

19th. That any person religiously scrupulous of bearing arms ought to be exempted upon payment of an equivalent to employ another to bear arms in his stead.

20th. That religion, or the duty which we owe to our Creator, and the manner of discharging it, can be directed only by reason and conviction, not by force or violence, and therefore all men have an equal, natural and unalienable right to the exercise of religion according to the dictates of conscience, and that no particular sect or society ought to be favored or established by law in preference to others.

[proposed] AMENDMENTS TO THE CONSTITUTION (as proposed by Virginia ratifying convention)

1st. That each state in the union shall respectively retain every power, jurisdiction and right, which is not by this constitution delegated to the Congress of the United States, or to the departments of the Foederal Government.

2d. That there shall be one representative for every thirty thousand, according to the enumeration or census mentioned in the Constitution, until the whole number of representatives amounts to two hundred; after which that number shall be continued or increased as Congress shall direct, upon the principles fixed in the Constitution, by apportioning the representatives of each state to some greater number of people from time to time as population increases.

3d. When Congress shall lay direct taxes or excises, they shall immediately inform the executive power of each state, of the quota of such state according to the census herein directed, which is proposed to be thereby raised; and if the legislature of any state shall pass a law which shall be effectual for raising such quota at the time required by Congress, the taxes and excises laid by Congress, shall not be collected in such state.

4th. That the members of the Senate and House of Representatives shall be ineligible to, and incapable of holding any civil office under the authority of the United States, during the time for which they shall respectively be elected.

5th. That the journals of the proceedings of the Senate and House of Representatives shall be published at least once in every year, except such parts thereof relating to treaties, alliances, or military operations, as in their judgment require secrecy.

6th. That a regular statement and account of the receipts and expenditures of all public money, shall be published at least once in every year.

7th. That no commercial treaty shall be ratified without the concurrence of two thirds of the whole number of the members of the Senate; and no treaty, ceding, contracting, or restraining or suspending the territorial rights or claims of the United States, or any of them, or their, or any of their rights or claims to fishing in the American seas, or navigating the American rivers, shall be made, but in cases of the most urgent and extreme necessity, nor shall any such treaty be ratified without the concurrence of three fourths of the whole number of the members of both houses respectively.

8th. That no navigation law or law regulating commerce shall be passed without the consent of two thirds of the members present, in both houses.

9th. That no standing army or regular troops shall be raised, or kept up in time of peace, without the consent of two thirds of the members present, in both houses.

10th. That no soldier shall be inlisted for any longer term than four years, except in time of war, and then for no longer term than the continuance of the war.

11th. That each state respectively shall have the power to provide for organizing, arming and disciplining its own militia, whensoever Congress shall omit or neglect to provide for the same. That the militia shall not be subject to martial law, except when in actual service in time of war, invasion or rebellion, and when not in the actual service of the United States, shall be subject only to such fines, penalties and punishments as shall be directed or inflicted by the laws of its own state.

12th. That the exclusive power of legislation given to Congress over the Foederal Town and its adjacent district, and other places purchased or to be purchased by Congress of any of the states, shall extend only to such regulations as respect the police and good government thereof.

13th. That no person shall be capable of being President of the United States for more than eight years in any term of sixteen years.

14th. That the judicial power of the United States shall be vested in one Supreme Court, and in such Courts of Admiralty as Congress may from time to time ordain and establish in any of the different states: The judicial power shall extend to all cases in law and equity arising under treaties made, or which shall be made under the authority of the United States; to all cases affecting ambassadors, other foreign ministers and consuls; to all cases of admiralty and maritime jurisdiction; to controversies to which the United States shall be a party; to controversies between two or more States, and between parties claiming lands under the grants of different States. In all cases affecting ambassadors, other foreign ministers and consuls, and those in which a state shall be a party, the Supreme Court shall have original jurisdiction; in all other cases before mentioned, the Supreme Court shall have appellate jurisdiction, as to matters of law only: except in cases of equity, and of admiralty and maritime jurisdiction, in which the Supreme Court shall have a appellate jurisdiction both as to law and fact, with such exceptions and under such regulations as the Congress shall make: But the judicial power of the United States

shall extend to no case where the cause of action shall have
originated before the ratification of this Constitution; except in
disputes between States about their territory; disputes between
persons claiming lands under the grants of different States, and suits
for debts due to the United States.

15th. That in criminal prosecutions, no man shall be restrained in the
exercise of the usual and accustomed right of challenging or
excepting to the jury.

16th. That Congress shall not alter, modify, or interfere in the times,
places, or manner of holding elections for Senators and
Representatives, or either of them, except when the Legislature of
any state shall neglect, refuse, or be disabled by invasion or rebellion
to prescribe the same.

17th. That those clauses which declare that Congress shall not
exercise certain powers, be not interpreted in any manner
whatsoever, to extend the powers of Congress; but that they be
construed either as making exceptions to the specified powers where
this shall be the case, or otherwise, as inserted merely for greater
caution.

18th. That the laws ascertaining the compensation of Senators and
representatives for their services, be postponed in their operation,
until after the election of representatives immediately succeeding the
passing thereof; that excepted, which shall first be passed on the
subject.

19th. That some tribunal other than the Senate be provided for trying
impeachments of Senators.

20th. That the salary of a judge shall not be increased or diminished
during his continuance in office otherwise than by general regulations
of salary, which may take place on a revision of the subject at stated
periods of not less than seven years, to commence from the same
such salaries shall be first ascertained by Congress.

AND the Convention do, in the name and behalf of the people of this
Commonwealth, enjoin it upon their representatives in Congress to

exert all their influence and use all reasonable and legal methods to obtain a **RATIFICATION** of the foregoing alterations and provisions in the manner provided by the fifth article of the said Constitution; and in all Congressional laws to be passed in the meantime, to conform to the spirit of these amendments as far as the said Constitution will admit.

Massachusetts Personal Liberty Act (1855)

Revised Statutes is hereby declared to be, that every person imprisoned or restrained of his liberty is entitled, as of right and of course, to the writ of habeas corpus, except in the cases mentioned in the second section of that chapter.

Sec. 3. The writ of habeas corpus may be issued by the supreme judicial court, the court of common pleas, by any justice's court or police court of any town or city, by any court of record, or by any justice of either of said courts, or by any judge of probate; and it may be issued by any justice of the peace, if no magistrate above named is known to said justice of the peace to be within five miles of the place where the party is imprisoned or restrained, and it shall be returnable before the supreme judicial court, or any one of the justices thereof, whether the court may be in session or not, and in term time or vacation...

Sec. 6. If any claimant shall appear to demand the custody or possession of the person for whose benefit such writ is sued out, such claimant shall state in writing the facts on which he relies, with precision and certainty; and neither the claimant of the alleged fugitive, nor any person interested in his alleged obligation to service or labor, nor the alleged fugitive, shall be permitted to testify at the trial of the issue; and no confessions, admissions or declarations of the alleged fugitive against himself shall be given in evidence. Upon every question of fact involved in the issue, the burden of proof shall be on the claimant, and the facts alleged and necessary to be established, must be proved by the testimony of at least two credible witnesses, or other legal evidence equivalent thereto, and by the rules of evidence known and secured by the common law; and no ex parte deposition or affidavit shall be received in proof in behalf of the claimant, and no presumption shall arise in favor of the claimant from any proof that the alleged fugitive or any of his ancestors had actually been held as a slave, without proof that such holding was legal.

Sec. 7. If any person shall remove from the limits of this Commonwealth, or shall assist in removing therefrom, or shall come into the Commonwealth with the intention of removing or of assisting in the removing therefrom, or shall procure or assist in procuring to be so removed, any person being in the peace thereof who is not held to service or labor by the party making claim, or who has not escaped from the party making claim, within the meaning of those words in the constitution of the United States, on the pretence that such person is so held or has so escaped, or that his service or labor is so due, or with the intent to subject him to such service or labor, he shall be punished by a fine of not less than one thousand, nor more than five thousand dollars, and by imprisonment in the State Prison not less than one, nor more than five years...

Sec. 9. No person, while holding any office of honor, trust, or emolument, under the laws of this Commonwealth, shall, in any capacity, issue any warrant or other process, or grant any certificate, under or by virtue of an act of congress . . . or shall in any capacity, serve any such warrant or other process.

Sec. 10. Any person who shall grant any certificate under or by virtue of the acts of congress, mentioned in the preceding section, shall be deemed to have resigned any commission from the Commonwealth which he may possess, his office shall be deemed vacant, and he shall be forever thereafter ineligible to any office of trust, honor or emolument under the laws of this Commonwealth.

Sec. 11. Any person who shall act as counsel or attorney for any claimant of any alleged fugitive from service or labor, under or by virtue of the acts of congress mentioned in the ninth section of this act, shall be deemed to have resigned any commission from the Commonwealth that he may possess, and he shall be thereafter incapacitated from appearing as counsel or attorney in the courts of this Commonwealth...

Sec. 14. Any person holding any judicial office under the constitution or laws of this Commonwealth, who shall continue, for ten days after the passage of this act, to hold the office of United States commissioner, or any office...which qualifies him to issue any warrant or other process...under the [Fugitive Slave Acts] shall be deemed to have violated good behavior, to have given reason for the loss of public confidence, and furnished sufficient ground either for impeachment or for removal by address.

Sec. 15. Any sheriff, deputy sheriff, jailer, coroner, constable, or other officer of this Commonwealth, or the police of any city or town, or any district, county, city or town officer, or any officer or other member of the volunteer militia of this Commonwealth, who shall hereafter arrest...any person for the reason that he is claimed or adjudged to be a fugitive from service or labor, shall be punished by fine...and by imprisonment...

Sec. 16. The volunteer militia of the Commonwealth shall not act in any manner in the seizure . . . of any person for the reason that he is claimed or adjudged to be a fugitive from service or labor...

Sec. 19. No jail, prison, or other place of confinement belonging to, or used by, either the Commonwealth of Massachusetts or any county therein, shall be used for the detention or imprisonment of any person accused or convicted of any offence created by [the Federal Fugitive Slave Acts]...or accused or convicted of obstructing or resisting any process, warrant, or order issued under either of said acts, or of rescuing, or attempting to rescue, any person arrested or detained under any of the provisions of either of the said acts.

NOTES

Preface

1. Jonah Goldberg of the National Review citing a Dan Aykroyd interview. Jonah Goldberg, "Incredible, Unstoppable Titan of Terror!" *National Review*, Feb. 3, 2003 (http://www.nationalreview.com/articles/205756/incredible-unstoppable-titan-terror/jonah-goldberg#)

2. "Obama Offers $3.8 Trillion Budget with Focus on Jobs," *Bloomberg*, Feb 1, 2010 (http://www.bloomberg.com/apps/news?pid=newsarchive&sid=aiHx BMm.6mgo) (May 28, 2012)

3. The White House Office of Management and Budget historical tables. (http://www.whitehouse.gov/omb/budget/Historicals) (May 28, 2012)

4. U.S. Tax Code (http://www.fourmilab.ch/uscode/26usc/)

5. OSHA Ladder specifications (http://www.osha.gov/pls/oshaweb/owadisp.show_document?p_tab le=standards&p_id=10839) (May 13, 2011)

6. "Largest-ever federal payroll to hit 2.15 million," *Washington Times,* Feb. 2, 2010 (http://www.washingtontimes.com/news/2010/feb/02/burgeoning-federal-payroll-signals-return-of-big-g/) (May 28, 2012)

7. "Federal Lands in the U.S.," *BigThink.com,* June 16, 2008 (http://bigthink.com/ideas/21343) (May 28, 2011)

Chapter 1

1. Gordon T. Belt, *Sedition Act of 1798 – A Brief History of Arrests, Indictments, Mistreatment & Abuse* First Amendment Center library (http://www.firstamendmentcenter.org/madison/wp-content/uploads/2011/03/Sedition_Act_cases.pdf)

2. Richard N. Rosenfeld, *American Aurora: A Democratic-Republican Returns*, (New York: St. Martin's Griffin, 1997), 80.

3. Carol Sue Humphrey, *The Revolutionary Era: Primary Documents on Events from 1776 to 1800*, (Westport, Connecticut: Greenwood Press, 2003), 325.

4. Rosenfeld, 526

5. Geoffrey R. Stone, *Perilous Times: Free Speech in Wartime, from the Sedition Act of 1798 to the War on Terrorism*, (New York: W.W. Norton & Company, Ltd., 2004), 54-56.

6. Ibid

7. Robert H. Churchill, *Manly Firmness, the Duty of Resistance, and the Search for a Middle Way: Democratic Republicans Confront the Alien and Sedition Acts,* (1999 Annual Meeting of the Society for

Historians of the Early American Republic, Lexington, Ky., July 17, 1999) (http://uhaweb.hartford.edu/CHURCHILL/SHEAR_Paper.pdf)

8. Newspaper article from the Kentucky Gazette dated 14 Nov. 1798

9. Churchill

10. Carol Sue Humphrey, *The Revolutionary Era: Primary Documents on Events from 1776 to 1800* (Westport, Connecticut: Greenwood Press (2003), 325.

11. Edward Everett, *The Writings and Speeches of Daniel Webster: Writings and speeches hitherto uncollected, v. 2. Speeches in Congress and diplomatic papers* (Google eBook, 1903), 68

12.   St. George Tucker, *View of the Constitution of the United States.* (Indianapolis, IN: Liberty Fund Inc., 1999), 121.

Chapter 2

1. *Obama on small-town Pa.: Clinging to religion, guns, xenophobia,* Politico.com, April 11, 2008 (http://www.politico.com/blogs/bensmith/0408/Obama_on_smallto wn_PA_Clinging_religion_guns_xenophobia.html) (May 28, 2012)

2. *CAGW Names Sen. John Kerry February Porker of the Month,* Reuters, Feb. 18, 2009 (http://www.reuters.com/article/2009/02/18/idUS246959+18-Feb-2009+BW20090218) (May 28, 2012)

3. *Pelosi to reporter: 'Are you serious?'* The Hill, Oct. 23, 2009 (http://thehill.com/blogs/blog-briefing-room/news/64547-pelosi-to-reporter-are-you-serious) (May 28, 2012)

4. Steve Benen, *Washington Monthly,* Sept. 1, 2009 (http://www.washingtonmonthly.com/archives/individual/2009_09/0 19724.php) (May, 28, 2012)

5. Frederick Bastiat, *The Law*

6. Angelo M. Codevilla, *America's Ruling Class – And the Perils of Revolution,* The American Spectator, July-Aug. 2010 issue (http://spectator.org/archives/2010/07/16/americas-ruling-class-and-the) (May 28, 2012)

7. John Locke, *Two Treatises of Government and A Letter Concerning Toleration*, edited by Ian Shapiro, (Yale University, 2003) *Second Treatise,* 101.

8. Tucker, 40.

9. Althusius 1995: 17 and 25

10. Locke, *Second Treatise,* 133

11. Locke used the word property in two ways. In this sense, he means everything a human being has sovereign control over – his life, his liberty (the freedom to act without coercion, or choose what authority we will submit to) and estate – physical things a person owns, ultimately as a result of his labor – specifically land. Locke often uses the word property in a more limited sense interchangeably with estate.

12. Locke, *Second Treatise,* 141-142

13. "And hence it is, that he who attempts to get any man into his absolute power, does thereby put himself in a state of war with him; it being to be understood as a declaration of a design upon his life: for I have reason to conclude, that he who would get me into his power without my consent, would use me as he pleased when he got me there, and destroy me too when he had a fancy to do it; for nobody can desire to have me in his absolute power, unless it be to compel me by force to that which is against the right of my freedom, i.e. make me a slave." Locke, *Second Treatise,* 107

Chapter 3

1. Althusius 1995: 115

2. Robert G. Natelson, *The Original Constitution: What it Actually Meant and Said*, (Los Angles: Tenth Amendment Center, 2010), 43.

3. Virginia ratifying convention speech of Henry Lee, June 9, 1788

4. Virginia ratifying convention speech of George Nichols, June 24, 1788

5. Stile – literally a step or set of steps use to cross over a fence or a wall. In this sense, it alludes to the "doorway" to ratification.

6. Virginia ratifying convention speech of Edmund Randolph, June 21, 1788

For an in depth look at the Virginia ratifying convention and its impact on our understanding of the Constitution, I highly recommend a paper by Kevin R. C. Gutzman (2004). *Edmund Randolph and Virginia Constitutionalism.* The Review of Politics, 66 , pp 469-498 doi:10.1017/S0034670500038870

Chapter 4

1. Benjamin Franklin, *On the Morals of Chess* (1779) (http://www.chess.com/forum/view/general/benjamin-franklin-on-the-morals-of-chess) (June 2, 2012)

2. Aristotle, *A Treatise on Government*, Book III, Chapter XVI (http://www.literaturepage.com/read/treatiseongovernment-104.html) (June 2, 2012)

3. Tucker, 28

4. Ibid, 31

5. James Madison letter to Henry Lee dated June 25, 1824. (http://rotunda.upress.virginia.edu/founders/default.xqy?keys=FOEA-print-02-02-02-0247) (June 2, 2012)

6. Thomas Jefferson, letter to William Johnson, dated June 12, 1823, *The Complete Jefferson*, 322.

7. Kevin R. C. Gutzman, *James Madison and the Making of America*, (New York: St. Martin's Press, 2012) Kindle version location 7027

8. Natelson, 19-24

9. Tucker, 105.

10. Ibid, 304-305

11. Natelson, 81-82

12. From Thomas Jefferson's opinion on the constitutionality of a national bank written February 15, 1791. (http://fearistyranny.wordpress.com/2008/08/17/thomas-jefferson-on-implied-powers-of-the-congress/) (June 2, 2012)

13. *The Debates in the Several State Conventions on the Adoption of the Federal Constitution, as Recommended by the General Convention at Philadelphia, in 1787*, (Jonathan Elliot ed., rev. 2d ed. 1941) (1836), 245-246.

14. Letter from James Madison to James Robertson dated April, 20, 1831

15. Letter from James Madison to Joseph C. Cabell dated Feb. 13, 1829 (http://press-pubs.uchicago.edu/founders/documents/a1_8_3_commerces19.html) (June 2, 2012)

16. Robert G. Natelson, *The Legal Meaning of "Commerce" in the Commerce Clause*, St. John's Law Review, Vol. 80:789 (2006)

(http://www.stjohns.edu/media/3/c8a62f91ae084a64b8aad2543dd1
72fc.pdf)

17. Randy E. Barnett, *The Original Meaning of the Commerce Clause*,
University of Chicago University of Chicago Law Review - Winter, 2001
- 68 U. Chi. L. Rev. 101

18. Ibid

19. Natelson, *Commerce*

Chapter 5

1. From one of the essays by Littleton Waller Tazewell appearing in
the Norfolk and Portsmouth Herald, compiled in *A Review of the
Proclamation of President Jackson*, 1833, (Norfolk, Va.: J.D. Ghiselin,
1888).

2. Tucker, 252

3. I shamelessly lifted this analogy from Tom Woods. He frequently
uses it in speeches. It's a lot funnier when he says it than it comes
across in writing!

4. John C. Calhoun, *The South Carolina Exposition and Protest (1828)*
(http://en.wikisource.org/wiki/South_Carolina_Exposition_and_Prote
st)

5. *South Carolina Ordinance of Nullification*
(http://en.wikisource.org/wiki/Ordinance_of_Nullification)

6. President Andrew Jackson address to Congress. It was delivered as
a speech on Dec. 4, 1832, but was sent to Congress in writing the day
before. (http://www.thisnation.com/library/sotu/1832aj.html)

7. Journal of the Senate, Friday, Jan. 11, 1833

8. Woods, Thomas E., *Nullification: How to Resist Federal Tyranny in the 21ˢᵗ Century* (Washington D.C.: Regency Publishing, Inc., 2010), 77.

9. Remini, Robert V., *Andrew Jackson and the Course of American Democracy, 1833-1845, v3* (1984), 42.

10. Madison's Notes On Nullification (1835) (http://oll.libertyfund.org/?option=com_staticxt&staticfile=show.php %3Ftitle=1940&chapter=119399&layout=html&Itemid=27)

11. Ibid

Chapter 6

1. You can watch the video at www.interviewwithazombie.com. Make sure you watch the blooper reel too. Absolutely hilarious!

2. Rachel Maddow, *Confederates in the Attic,* MSNBC April 12, 2011. (http://www.youtube.com/watch?v=vK8O3I0NXQQ)

3. See H. Robert Baker, *The Rescue of Joshua Glover: A Fugitive Slave, the Constitution, and the Coming of the Civil War* (Athens, OH: Ohio University Press, 2006), 122

4. *Declaration of the Immediate Causes Which Induce and Justify the Secession of South Carolina from the Federal Union* (Dec. 24, 1860) (http://avalon.law.yale.edu/19th_century/csa_scarsec.asp)

5. *Fugitive Slave Act of 1850* (http://www.nationalcenter.org/FugitiveSlaveAct.html)

6. *Introduction To The Massachusetts Personal Liberty Act* (http://eca.state.gov/education/engteaching/pubs/AmLnC/br20.htm)

7. Michigan liberty law. http://www.michigan.gov/dnr/0,4570,7-153-54463_18670_44390-160662--,00.html

8. The primary source for the account of Joshua Glover's escape from slavery comes from *Finding Freedom: The Untold Story of Joshua Glover, Runaway Slave,* by Ruby West Jackson and Walter T. McDonald (Madison, WI: Wisconsin Historical Society Press, 2007). Additional information comes from Thomas Wood's *Nullification.* He sources Baker.

9. *Eyes on the Prize: America's Civil Rights Years (1954–1965),* PBS documentary released in 1987

10. *Rosa Parks: My Story* (Pufin Books, 1999)

Chapter 7

1. Most of the info on Kudzu was taken from, *The Amazing Story of Kudzu* (http://www.maxshores.com/kudzu/). Some sourced from Wikipedia as well.

2. Iowa Republican Straw Poll debate, Ames, Iowa, Aug. 11, 2011 (http://www.issues2000.org/Archive/2011_Straw_Poll_Rick_Santorum.htm) (June 4, 2012)

3. Frederick Bastiat, *The Law* (1850), Kindle edition

4. *Final Report of the Tuskegee Syphilis Study Legacy Committee1— May 20, 1996* – University of Virginia Claude Moore Health Sciences Library. (http://www.hsl.virginia.edu/historical/medical_history/bad_blood/report.cfm) (June 4, 2012)

5. Woods, 18

6. Able P. Upshur, *A Brief Enquiry into the True Nature and Character of Our Federal Government: Being a Review of Judge Story's Commentaries on the Constitution of the United States* (New York: Van Evrie, Horton & Co., 1868) Kindle edition.

7. *Semiannual Report of the War Relocation Authority, for the period January 1 to June 30, 1946*, not dated. Papers of Dillon S. Myer. Scanned images at www.trumanlibrary.org.

8. Mary Tsukamoto quote: http://americanhistory.si.edu/ourstory/activities/internment/more.html Retrieved March 11, 2012

9. *Mein Kampf* (http://www.greatwar.nl/books/meinkampf/meinkampf.pdf) (June 4, 2012)

10. William Sharp McKechnie, *Magna Carta: A Commentary on the Great Charter of King John, with an Historical Introduction.* (http://oll.libertyfund.org/?option=com_staticxt&staticfile=show.php%3Ftitle=338&chapter=48697&layout=html&Itemid=27)

11. McLynn, Frank. *Lionheart and Lackland: King Richard, King John and the Wars of Conquest.* (London: Vintage Books, 2007)

12. Immanuel Kant, *Groundwork for the Metaphysics of Morals* (Edited and translated by Mary Gregor, Cambridge. (1998) 42-43.

13. Woods, Thomas E., *Rollback: Repealing Big Government Before the Coming Fiscal Collapse,* (Washington D.C.: Regency Publishing Inc., 2011) Kindle edition

Chapter 8

1. *2008 campaign costliest in U.S. history*, Politco.com, Nov. 5, 2008. (http://www.politico.com/news/stories/1108/15283.html) (June 4, 2012)

2. OpenSecrets.org lobbying database
(http://www.opensecrets.org/lobby/) (Jun 4, 2012)

3. *Only 10 percent turn out to cast their votes*, Lexington Herald-Leader, May 18, 2011
(http://www.kentucky.com/2011/05/18/1743259/no-waiting-at-most-precincts.html)

4. *Federal aid is top revenue for states*, USA Today, May 4, 2009
(http://www.usatoday.com/news/nation/2009-05-04-fed-states-revenue_N.htm)

5. From a report I wrote for the Tenth Amendment Center:

AUSTIN, Texas (June 20, 2011) – On Monday, Texas Gov. Rick Perry presented legislation for consideration in the ongoing Eighty-Second Texas Legislature, First Called Session that would ban intrusive TSA pat-downs.

NOW, THEREFORE, I, RICK PERRY, *Governor of the State of Texas, by the authority vested in me by Article IV, Section 8, and Article III, Section 40, of the Texas Constitution, do hereby present the following subject matter to the Eighty-Second Texas Legislature, First Called Session, for consideration:*

Legislation relating to prosecution and punishment for the offense of official oppression of persons seeking access to public buildings and transportation.

The move comes after a videotaped discussion at a book signing between a Texas resident and the governor went viral. In the widely circulated YouTube video, Perry indicated that he would not present the TSA bill unless there were enough votes in the House and Senate for passage. When the constituent indicated the support existed, Perry acted surprised and then went on to say he didn't think there was enough time to get the legislation passed.

Bill author David Simpson (R-Longwood) released an open letter to Perry Monday morning, pleading with the governor to get the bill on the agenda.

"Texans overwhelmingly support this measure as I am sure your office can attest. And the Legislature is ready to pass it as soon as you call the bill," Simpson wrote. "Governor Perry, there remains only for you to call the bill. Any concerns for time would be quickly wiped away if you would take the bull by the horns and provide leadership on this bill."

The bill will move forward in the Special Session as HB 41.

ABOUT THE AUTHOR

Mike Maharrey serves as the national communications director for the Tenth Amendment Center. He earned a B.A. in Mass Communications and Media Studies with an emphasis in news and editorial journalism at the University of South Florida St. Petersburg in 2008, and covered state and local politics for several newspapers, including the St. Petersburg Times and the Kentucky Gazette. He worked for two years as the sports editor for a community newspaper and won two Kentucky Press Association awards for in 2009. While working toward his degree, Mike played two seasons for the USF Ice Bulls and earned American Collegiate Hockey Association Academic All-American honors in 2008 at the ripe young age of 40. He also earned a B.S. in Accounting from the University of Kentucky in 1991. Mike lives in Lexington, Ky. and is working with his wife Cynthia to raise three teenagers. In his spare time, Mike still enjoys stopping some pucks and studying history.

ABOUT THE TENTH AMENDMENT CENTER

The TAC is a national think-tank based in Los Angeles, California. Founded in 2006 in response to what was seen as continual violations of the Constitution by both major political parties, the Center is dedicated to a short, but very straightforward mission:

The Constitution.
Every issue, every time. No exceptions, no excuses.

Made in the USA
Charleston, SC
08 February 2014